de Voltregà
Emb. de Sau
Emb. d'el Pasteral
Sant Gregori
1091
Iberico
Mare de Déu dels Angels
Aiguafreda
Begur
R. Ter
Anglès
Quart d'Onyar
La Bisbal
Vic
R. Mayor
Emb. de Susqueda
R. Osor
Sta. Barbara
R. Daró
Tamariu
Palafrugell
Sant Julià de Vilatorta
SA. DE LES GAVARRES
Puig d' Arques
531
Cap de Sant Sebastià
Sant Hilari Sacalm
Sta. Coloma de Farners
Cassà de la Selva
Calonge
Tona
Sta. Coloma
Palamós
SERRA DEL MONTSENY
Arbúcies
Llagostera
Moià
R. Congost
Sils
Sta. Cristina d'Aro
La Platja d'Aro
Turó de l'Home
1709
Montseny
Hostalric
Sant Feliu de Guíxols
Rosamar
Sant Miquel del Fai
PARC NATURAL DEL MONTSENY
R. Tordera
Tossa
Sant Celoni
Tordera
COSTA BRAVA
Sant Feliu de Codines
La Garriga
Lloret de Mar
Blanes
Montnegre
R. Tenes
Caldes de Montbui
El Corredor
638
Arenys de Munt
Malgrat de Mar
Granollers
Sant Pol de Mar
Sabadell
Arenys de Mar
Argentona
Mollet
Mataró
COSTA MARESME
Mediterranean Sea
Cerdanyola
Montcada
Vilassar de Mar
Sant Cugat del Vallès
Montgat
Badalona
Tibidabo
Barcelona
Montjuïc
Costa Br
12 km / 7.5 miles

Spain
160 km / 100 miles
Atlantic
Ocean
C. Ortegal
El Ferrol
La Coruña
C. Finisterre
Gijón
Oviedo
Lugo
CORDILLERA
CANTABRICA
León
Orense
Vigo
Santander
Bilbao
San Sebastián
Bayonne
FRANCE
Toulouse
Montpellier
Nîmes
Sète
Carcassonne
Pau
Tarbes
PYRENEES
Pamplona
Logroño
ANDORRA
Perpignan
C. Creus
Girona
Terrassa
Barcelona
Lérida
Zaragoza
Burgos
Soria
Bellavente
Valladolid
Duero
Braga
Porto
Douro
Salamanca
Calatayud
Ebro
Tarragona
Tortosa
ESPANA
(SPAIN)
Segovia
Aveiro
Guarda
Madrid
Alcalá de Henares
Teruel
Coimbra
Castelo Branco
Cuenca
Toledo
Leiria
Tajo
Tejo
Santarém
Cáceres
Lisboa
PORTUGAL
Badajoz
Ciudad Real
Guadiana
Júcar
Albacete
Castellón de la Plana
Valencia
C. de la Nao
Almadén
Valdepeñas
Setúbal
Evora
Zafra
SIERRA MORENA
Beja
Córdoba
Jaén
Guadalquivir
Murcia
Alicante
Elx
Cartagena
Sevilla
Huelva
Lagos
Faro
C. de S. Vicente
Jerez de la Frontera
Cádiz
SIERRA NEVADA
Granada
Águilas
Almería
C. de Gata
Málaga
Strait of Gibraltar
Gibraltar
Tarifa
Tanger
Ceuta (Sp.)
Tétouan
Larache
MOROCCO
Melilla (Sp.)
Mediterranean
Sea
MENORCA
MALLORCA
Palma
IBIZA
FORMENTERA
ISLAS BALEARES
(BALEARIC ISLANDS)
Algier
Blida
Ech Cheliff
Mostaganem
Oran
Tlemcen
Chott El Hodna
ALGERIA
ISLAS CANARIAS (SP).
(CANARY ISLANDS)
LA PALMA
TENERIFE
Sta. Cruz de Tenerife
GOMERA
HIERRO
GRAN CANARIA
Las Palmas
FUERTEVENTURA
LANZAROTE

INSIGHT POCKET GUIDES

Costa Brava

Author	**Roger Williams**
Publisher	**Hans Höfer**
Design Concept	**V Barl**
Designer	**Karen Hoisington**
Photographer	**Roger Williams**
Managing Editor	**Christopher Catling**

INSIGHT POCKET GUIDES

Insight Pocket Guide:

COSTA BRAVA

Directed by
Hans Höfer

Managing Editor
Andrew Eames

Photography by
Roger Williams

Design Concept by
V. Barl

Design by
Karen Hoisington

Printed in Singapore by
Höfer Press (Pte) Ltd
Fax: 65-8616438

Distributed in the UK & Ireland by
GeoCenter International UK Ltd
The Viables Center, Harrow Way
Basingstoke, Hampshire RG22 4BJ
ISBN: 9-62421-533-2

Worldwide distribution enquiries:
Höfer Communications Pte Ltd
38 Joo Koon Road
Singapore 2262
ISBN: 9-62421-533-2

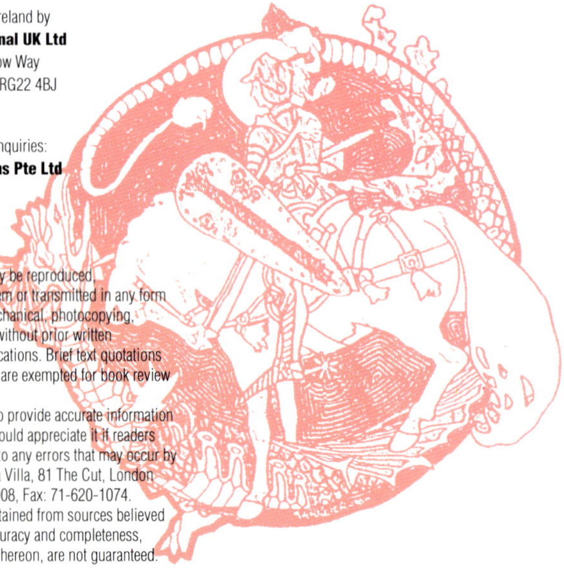

As every effort is made to provide accurate information in this publication, we would appreciate it if readers would call our attention to any errors that may occur by communicating with Apa Villa, 81 The Cut, London SE1 8LL. Tel: 71-620-0008, Fax: 71-620-1074. Information has been obtained from sources believed to be reliable, but its accuracy and completeness, and the opinions based thereon, are not guaranteed.

Benvinguts

Welcome! I first visited Costa Brava following in the footsteps of medieval pilgrims; my object was to seek out the remote churches of the Pyrenees, rugged Romanesque buildings often located in flower-filled mountain pastures. Since then I have bought a house in the region to which I escape with my family whenever I need to get away from the pressures of a journalistic life. The Costa Brava is one of Europe's fabled shores. It lies in Catalonia, in the north-east corner of Spain. Between Barcelona and the Pyrenean border with France is the province of Girona, where the coast is *brava:* rugged and wild. It is a beautiful place, of cliffs and coves and sandy beaches, and it has proved irresistible to writers, poets and artists. It has also attracted tourists, and hundreds of hotels and apartments were hastily put up to make the most of the demand, which has slackened in recent years. Yet it is wrong to think the coast is nothing but a promenade backed by concrete hotels. Surrounded by the scent of stone pines, fishing villages can still be idyllic, and bays and inlets can seem as timeless and remote as they did to the Greeks and Romans.

Resorts often display a 'welcome' sign. The word for welcome is not *bienvenido* as in Spanish nor the French *bienvenue*, but the Catalan *benvinguts*. Catalonia is a buffer zone between Spain and France, being not quite one, not quite the other. Life is a mix of each: a Mediterranean enthusiasm which does not embrace a love of flamenco or bullfighting; an afternoon siesta does not tarnish a reputation for thrift and hard work; an abundance of cheap wine does not lead to drunkenness. The new generation of holiday-makers here want more than just sun, sea and cheap wine. In my years here I have discovered that the region has a great deal to offer, as I hope my insider's guide to the coast and its unspoiled inland regions shows.

Welcome! Benvinguts! — Roger Williams

Contents

Preceding pages: The Costa from Sant Pere de Rodes, Cap de Creus

Following pages: Sun and sea near Sant Feliu

CRUCEROS

The Olympic Connection

Cap de Creus, the last craggy outcrop of the Pyrenees in the north of the Costa Brava, lies at the top of the Bay of Roses. This is where Greek traders settled around 550BC. They put down roots at Empúries, which means emporium or trading place, and named the Bay of Roses after the island of Rhodes.

Three centuries later the region was an important part of the Carthaginian empire. Hamil Barca gave his name to Barcelona and his son, Hannibal, started out from here when he took his elephants over the Pyrenees to launch an attack on Italy in 218BC. To cut off Hannibal's supply line, Scipio landed with an army at Empúries in the same year; in 195BC the consul Cato began the systematic subjugation of the peninsula from here. A new town (Neapolis) was

Tossa de Mar

e Culture

built alongside the old Greek one (Palaeopolis). The foundations of both are still visible and this impressive site was chosen as the point for the torch, carried from Olympia, to come ashore in 1992 for the Barcelona Games.

For 600 years, the Roman influence was strong and they left a lasting legacy. There is little difference between the ancient Roman style of country villas – sturdy, square, two-storey buildings with baked tiles on sloping roofs – and the traditional Catalan farmhouses, *masies*, which could have been built at any time in the past 2,000 years. The Romans also bequeathed to Catalonia its language. Christianity came to the region with the Visigoths; King Reccared finally converted to Roman Christianity in AD587, an act he celebrated by building a church at Ripoll, a mountain town tucked in the Ter valley north-west of Girona (see Tour 12: *Cradle of Catalonia*).

Following the death of Mohammed the Berber tribes of North Africa, fired with Muslim holy zeal, crossed the Straits of Gibraltar in AD711 and drove up through Spain, reaching Catalonia after six years. Muslim occupation of Catalonia was comparatively short, lasting less than 100 years, and virtually nothing remains of their time here (the 'Arab baths' in Girona were built more than 400 years later). Nor was there any time for them to influence the language, which they certainly did in the rest of Spain.

Catalonia then became part of a buffer zone, running the length of the Pyrenees, separating the Muslims to the south from Christian Europe to the north. The region was ruled by Guifré el Pilós (Wilfred the Hairy). A fanciful tale all Catalan children are taught is that Guifré was wounded while fighting alongside Charles the Bald (the King of the Franks and grandson of Charlemagne). Charles dipped his fingers in Guifré's blood and wiped them down his golden shield, thus giving Guifré a grant of arms and designing the *quatre barres*, the red-and-yellow striped flag of Catalonia, which is one of the oldest in Europe.

In AD897 Guifré died fighting the Moors in the neighbouring province of Lleida and was buried in the Monastery of Santa Maria he had built on the site of Reccared's church at Ripoll, today called 'the cradle of Catalonia'. The family dynasty he founded, the House of Barcelona, went on to rule Catalonia for 500 years.

The Flowering of Romanesque

While crusaders and counts fought to reconquer Spain from the Muslims, Catalonia was left in relative peace and Benedictine monks presided over the extraordinary flowering of culture that began here in the 11th century. In this corner of Catalonia, Abbot Oliba led the way. As bishop of Vic he built the first shrine to the Black Virgin at Montserrat, Catalonia's holy mountain, west of Barcelona, as well as initiating extensive building works in his own cathedral.

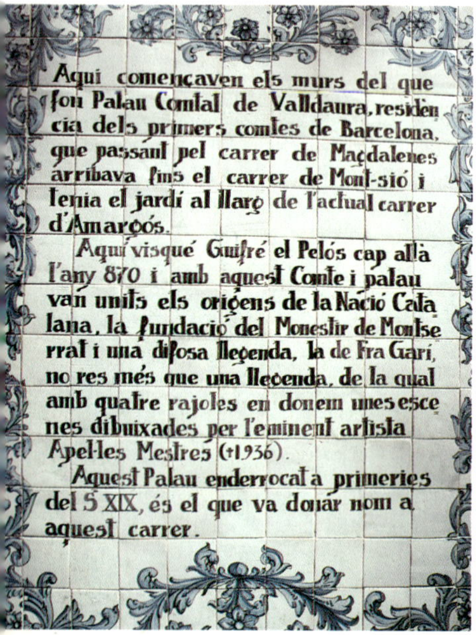

Most of all, however, Oliba is associated with Guifré's monastery at Ripoll where he was abbot from 1008 to 1046. He brought it to physical greatness, and gave it a reputation as a formidable place of learning, with a fine library of illuminated manuscripts. Through Ripoll's portals, the most magnificent carved stonework of the period, much Islamic scientific and mathematical knowledge was passed to the West, including it is thought, our Arabic numerals.

A Great Maritime Power

Nearly every town and village in the province has either a statue to, or a street named after Jaume I, el Conqueridor (James the Conqueror), who reigned for 63 years from 1213. He began Catalonia's seaborne expansion, taking Mallorca and Ibiza from the Moors in 1229. Jaume made Catalan the country's official language and he wrote of his exploits in his *Llibre de Feits*, the first of four outstanding Catalan historical documents, known as the *Chronicles*. Expansion continued under Jaume's successor, Pere II, el Gran (Peter the Great, 1276–85), who was assisted by the famous admiral, Roger de Llúria. De Llúria gave Catalonia virtually a clean sweep of the western Mediterranean, proving its superiority in a notable encounter with the French in 1285.

As Catalonia's influence spread, so did its language, dispersed by conquerers, traders, troubadors and scholars. The most influential writer was the theologian, philosopher, poet and tireless traveller Ramon Llull who was born in Mallorca in 1232, three years after Jaume had taken it from the Moors. He produced the first vernacular translation of the Bible, in his native Catalan. In 1395 a literary competition was held in Barcelona. It was called the *Jocs Florals*, the Flower Games, because flowers were awarded to the winners. The games were a high point of a culture which was rich, powerful and civilised, and nearly 500 years later the games were revived as a potent symbol of the continuity of that civilisation.

Decline

Catalonia's decline really began as the rest of Spain consolidated and prospered. In 1479 Fernando of Catalonia-Aragón married Isabella of Castile, uniting the two great Spanish houses. More than that, the 'Catholic monarchs' united the whole peninsula when they drove the last of the Moors from the south.

The Corts, or Catalan parliament, continued to hold onto its rights, but there were continual arguments with Madrid. Throughout the Thirty Years' War with France, Catalonia was treated as a sacrificial pawn. Spanish mercenary forces were billeted on the people, until their resentment against Spanish repression finally boiled over, resulting in a riot in Barcelona on the feast of Corpus Christi, 1640. Catalans still see the revolt in Barcelona as one of their finest hours, and the song of the harvesters who led the uprising, *Els Segadors*, has become their national anthem.

Catalonia could not get away with bucking Madrid again. When Felipe V, founder of the Bourbon dynasty, was crowned King of Spain, he took revenge on Catalonia for supporting rival claimants

Sculpted façade from Santa Maria, Castelló d'Empúries

Catalan wall tiles showing crafts and industries

to the throne. The *Decreto de Nueva Planta* was a vengeful, Draconian decree, designed to teach Catalonia a lesson once and for all. Laws, privileges, institutions were all abolished. Books were burned and the Catalan language banned from official use.

Crushed, but not defeated, Catalonia eventually settled down to a time of hard work and expansion. The region's fast-flowing Pyrenean rivers were harnessed to drive forges, turning Catalonia into a centre for iron and armaments manufacture. When cotton began to arrive from the Americas, the waters proved ideal for fabric production, and the Olot School of Fine Art was founded to create new fabric designs. By the middle of the 19th century the region had led the country's industrial revolution and become the powerhouse of Spain. Cork production became a boom industry on the coast and helped to finance the building of Spain's first railway, running up the coast from Barcelona to Mataró, with branch lines to the cork capitals of Palafrugell and Sant Feliu.

The *Renaixença*

Railways also headed for the mountains and Catalans climbed aboard them in search of their roots. *The Renaixença*, a romantic movement, had begun. Like the Rissorgimento in Spain, or Frédéric Mistral's attempted revival of Provençal, it looked back to the past, when Catalan was the language of Mediterranean traders and troubadors, and Catalonia ruled the waves.

In 1859, the romantically inspired *literati* of Barcelona revived the *Jocs Florals* of the troubadors. One of its early winners was a young priest, Jacint Verdaguer, who was born near Vic in 1845. A popular and inspirational writer, he led the language back to the printed page. One of Verdaguer's patriotic epics is called *Canigó* after the great snowy mountain which actually lies just inside France, but which overlooks much of Catalonia. In Verdaguer's poem, the mountain becomes a symbol of the nation's hope and endurance, and since Franco's death there has been a revival of the midsummer fires of St John, when runners carry torches down from

The defence of Girona, 1809

its summit to various corners of Catalonia on both sides of the border.

Verdaguer's *Canigó* encouraged Catalans to look to their own land. Inspired by their poets, aided by the railways and propelled by a new found prosperity, people flocked to the countryside, seeking snowy peaks, remote valleys, and curative spas. And, as elsewhere in Europe, they began to discover the pleasures of the seaside.

The Civil War and After

Artistic and cultural life in Catalonia in the early 20th century was inextricably tied up with the dream, shared by both traditionalists and progressives, of independence from Spain. The aspirations of the Catalans to achieve autonomy made them natural supporters of the Republican cause during the Spanish Civil War and the area suffered as a consequence. As Franco's Nationalist army moved up from the south, the Costa Brava was bombed from the air and heavy shells were fired from Italian ships based in Mallorca. Pillboxes and gun emplacements hastily built on hill and cliff tops are still there, incongruous among the white villas. The Nationalist army entered Barcelona on 26 January. Girona fell on 5 February, and the Nationalists pushed past Olot and Ripoll towards the Pyrenees. The Republican government convened for the last time in the pentagonal fortress at Figueres.

Franco was in power for nearly two generations. The Civil War had been horrendous, but thoughts of democracy and *catalanisme* did not go away. There were protests from local heroes such as Lluís Llach, a folk singer from Verges, who still often joins in the annual Dance of Death held in the town on Maundy Thursday.

The death of Franco in 1975 came as a great relief, particularly when King Juan Carlos, who had been groomed by Franco to take over, turned out to be a democrat. The Catalan parliament, the Generalitat, was re-established and semi-autonomy was granted to Catalonia, as it was to other restless peoples. The language returned quickly: thousands of volumes were published some winning prizes. Radio and TV stations broadcast in Catalan. Road signs were rewritten. Schools began teaching in Catalan, with Spanish as a second language.

Exile at the end of the Civil War

The Tourism Phenomenon

In *Voices from the Old Sea*, the English writer Norman Lewis describes the three summer seasons between 1949 and 1951 when tourists began to arrive at a small Costa Brava fishing village. He called the village Farol, because he did not want the villagers, or the village, identified and embarrassed. The life of a Costa Brava fisherman, as he described it, was medieval. It was riven with superstition: no-one wore leather; nets for the tunny fish would only be cast when the medicine man arrived; old people might take to their beds for the whole winter. In an inland village dogs sniffed around the corpse of a man who had starved in the streets. In the bars, fishermen talked in verse. The book did not go down well with some local politicians. The Costa Brava, they said, was not 'discovered' by tourists after the last war. It had been named the *costa brava*, the 'wild coast', by a local journalist, Ferran Agulló, back in 1911. By 1928 a regular weekly bus was running from Berlin to Tossa de Mar, which had a sophisticated summer season.

Nevertheless, it was not until the post-war period that tourists began to arrive in significant numbers. Those who came in the 1950s found this coast both beautiful and staggeringly cheap. Word quickly got around. The Girona-Costa Brava charter-only airport was opened during the economic boom of the 1960s. Whole new towns, such as Empúria-brava and La Platja D'Aro grew up beside welcoming sandy beaches. Cost conscious package-tour operators demanded the cheapest possible accommodation for their clients. That's exactly what they got.

Now, in the early 1990s, the region is adapting to yet another change. Package holidays are no longer as popular and new developments have been halted. The area is once again attracting the more sophisticated travellers and is leading the way in terms of conservation. Green belts have been established, the wetlands of Aiguamolls turned into a bird sanctuary and the Medes Islands made into Spain's first marine nature reserve.

HISTORY

BC

550 Ancient Greek traders establish the port of Empúries.

218 Hannibal launches the Second Punic War and the Roman general Scipio Africanus invades Empúries in retaliation.

195 Romans embark on a succesful campaign to conquer Spain and rule the peninsula for the next six centuries.

AD

5th century After the collapse of Roman rule, Catalonia is occupied by the Visigoths.

587 The Visigothic King Reccared converts to Christianity.

711 North African Muslims invade the Spanish mainland.

717 Catalonia is occupied by the Muslims.

778 Charlemagne begins a campaign to drive the Moors out of northern Spain.

9th century Catalonia, freed from Moorish rule, becomes part of a buffer zone under Frankish authority.

897 Death of Guifré el Pilós, founder of the House of Barcelona; under successive Counts of Barcelona, Catalonia becomes a prosperous independent principality.

11th–15th centuries The flowering of Benedictine monasticism and of the Catalan Romanesque style of architecture.

1276 Death of Jaume I, the Conqueror under whom Catalonia reached the limits of its expansion and among other things, became a major maritime power.

1479 Marriage of Fernando and Isabella, the 'Catholic monarchs', responsible for unifying Spain, having driven the Moors from the country.

1492 Christopher Columbus sets sail for the Americas.

June 1640 Revolt of the Segadors (harvesters) against Spanish exploitation of Catalonia during the Thirty Years' War with France.

1716 Catalonia suffers heavily for supporting the losing side in the Spanish War of Succession. Felipe V's *Decreto de Nueva Planta* abolishes Catalan law, language and institutions.

1778 Catalonia is allowed to trade with the Americas (previously the monopoly of Seville and Cadiz). Exports of cork and imports of cotton are the basis of Catalonia's expanding economy.

1848 Spain's first railway is built in Catalonia, by now the country's leading manufacturer.

1859 Revival of the *Jocs Florals* literary festival, the beginning of Catalan cultural reawakening.

1888 Barcelona's Universal Exhibition, a celebration of Catalan industrial and economic achievement, and the first showcase of the *Modernista* architectural style.

1936 Start of the Spanish Civil War.

1960s Beginning of the Costa Brava package-tour boom.

1975 Death of General Franco and the dawn of a new era of Catalan semi-autonomy.

1983 Creation of Aiguamolls natural park.

1985 The Medes Islands become Spain's first marine nature reserve.

1986 Spain's entry to the European Community brings many benefits to the region.

1992 Olympic Games held in Barcelona, resulting in major investment and infrastructural improvements.

Tour Selec

The Costa Brava region looks deceptively small on a map. As the crow flies, the Costa Brava stretches for 58 miles (93.3km) from the French border just above Portbou to the point where it joins Barcelona's Maresme coast just south of Blanes. By road, however, the shortest distance is 98 miles (157.7km) from north to south and the coastline itself, with its numerous bays and inlets, capes and headlands, actually measures over 200 miles (321.8km). Bear this in mind when planning a visit to the Costa Brava. A car is essential for touring the region and account must be taken of the time it takes to travel from one destination to another; places that do not look far apart take longer to reach because of the way the roads plunge inland from the coast and back again.

The routes in this guide start in the north, at Figueres, and then work southwards, through Girona, the provincial capital, to Blanes, the southernmost resort on the Costa Brava. From here, the tours take you inland and northwards through the mountainous region of Montseny, to Vic, Ripoll and Olot. These inland tours will show you a different face of the region to the one on the coast.

If you rent a coastal villa for the duration of your stay, you will find that all of the destinations in this guide are closer than two hours' drive away and are often less, depending on where you are based. Alternatively, you can follow the routes in sequence, stopping off for the night along the way in one of the region's numerous *hostals* or *pensiós*. The routes have been deliberately designed not to be over-taxing. Some of the tours ask you specifically to set out early in the day. The benefits of following this advice include empty beaches, no queues at shops or museums and less travelling when the sun is hot.

tions

Figueres

1. Dalí's Town

Your first day in the Costa Brava region should be a relaxing one, getting to know Figueres, a typical Catalan town, with its renowned Dalí Museum.

Figueres lies on the main N-II road 20 miles (32km) north of Girona. The capital of the High Empordà is a thorough-going

The Dalí Museum in Figueres

Catalan town. Its most famous son has put it on the tourist map. Salvador Dalí's museum in the former theatre is the most popular in Spain after the Prado in Madrid. A visit to the town could be combined with a concert at nearby Vilabertran or Peralada, although these start late. In between, a meal at the Duran Hotel or the Hotel Ampurdan, fount of modern Catalan cuisine, would make the evening additionally memorable. If at all possible, go on a Thursday which is market day.

The **Dalí Museum** is easily found among the pedestrianised shopping lanes off the Rambla (daily, 10am–6pm; entrance fee). In high season avoid queues by going early in the morning or around lunchtime, having spent the morning in the markets or shops. The museum is full of visual and surrealist jokes. Children will love it.

Figueres's most famous son, Salvador Dalí, was born in the county town of the High Empordà in 1904. His father was a local notary, and a firm of lawyers in the Rambla still has on its shelves books of legal documents which are signed with his elaborate flourish. The local theatre, built in 1850, fell into disrepair in the 1936–9 Civil War, but was given to Dalí for his museum in the 1970s. It is now firmly established as one of Europe's great museums. Dalí spent the last few incapacitated years of his life in an apartment built into the museum, but he is also associated with

Portlligat, a delightful cove on the edge of Cap de Creus, where he and his wife Gala lived and held court in two renovated fishermen's cottages (see Tour 2). For lunch you can eat inexpensively in typical local style at the nearby **El Gallo Rojo**, in Carrer de les Bruixes, or at **Can Jeroni**, a small restaurant in Carrer Castelló, which runs out of the top left corner of the Plaça del Gra.

Charcuterie at the Thursday market

The **Toy Museum** (Museu de Joguets), in the old Hotel Paris in the Rambla, is the next place to visit. Its rooms contain a good collection of toys from all over the world and they have a nostalgia value for adults as well as being great fun for children. A couple of minutes' walk down from here, at the bottom of the Rambla, is the **Museum of the Empordà**, which has a collection of odds and ends from around the region. Visit it if there is time; entrance is free.

The cafés in the **Rambla** are pleasant to sit out in. Try a real chocolate drink (*xocolata*) or almond milk (*orxata*) at the old Royal. Smaller children can enjoy the swings and slides in the park, where there is also a café. To find it, go to the top of the Rambla, turn right and then left up Carrer Pep Ventura. Ventura (1817–75), inventor of the modern form of the *sardana* (Catalan music and dance), is another of Figueres's favourite sons and there is a statue to him in the Plaça Josep Tarradellas. The statue at the bottom of the Rambla however, is to another local hero, Narcís Monturiol (1819–85), the inventor of the submarine.

Shopping is good in Figueres. In Carrer Pep Ventura is a cavernous antique shop, **Quintana**. Smarter shops line the Rambla, continuing down to Plaça de la Palmera, where the new **Granja Maia**, though cold and modern looking, has delicious bread. At the top of the Rambla on the left is **Masdevall**, a bookshop full of local publications, and **Carrer Vilafant**, the road to the left, leads to some interesting greengrocers which always have seasonal wild mushrooms.

Best of all is the Thursday market, which is divided into two parts. There is a food market under cover in **Plaça del Gra** on the Roses side of the town, and linen, hardware, toys, shoes and clothes in **Passeig Nou** by the park on the inland side. There is also a daily indoor fish market at the bottom of the Rambla, situated in the **Plaça Escorxador**.

Pep Ventura's statue

2. Two Sunrises Over Cap de Creus

Breakfast at dawn at the castle of Sant Salvador; anchovy boats at El Port de la Selva; lunch and a leisurely afternoon in Cadaqués; Dali's home in Portlligat.

In that time the Spaniards call *madrugada*, the hour before dawn, take a flask of coffee and a bag of *madalenas* (small sponge cakes) and head across the High Empordà to the **Monastery of Sant Pere de Rodes**. A road behind the village of Vilajuiga takes about 20mins to wind up the Verdera mountains towards this Romanesque glory nestling just beneath the 2,205ft (672m) summit. The car park is free at this time of day; the last half mile has to be walked.

The monastery, dating from the 9th century, is magnificent. Built on the site of a Roman temple to Venus Pyrenea, it commanded most of the considerable land it surveys. It doesn't open to the public until 10am, but there is enough to see. Don't linger. Take the path to the right of the entrance, which leads, after 25mins, to the **castle of Sant Salvador** at the summit of what is effectively the Pyrenees' last shrug before diving into the sea. This is the spot to watch the sun come up. From the walls of this ruined fortress there is a fabulous 360° view across to the Pyrenees and **Mt Canigó**, Catalonia's spiritual heart, over the Empordà plain and the great sweep of the Bay of Roses, and out over Cap de Creus to the sea.

Beneath lies **El Port de la Selva** and it takes 20mins to drive down to its shallow waters, which may still be in the shadow of the hills behind the town on the far side of the bay. If it is, the sun will soon seem to rise for the second time. Cool off with a dip: no-one will be swimming at this hour and fish will swim around your feet. Have a coffee and croissant in the **Marina**, the first bar in town to open. When the anchovy boats are here they bring in their night's catch, towing their small lamp-carrying boats, at about 9am.

The Romanesque monastery of Sant Pere de Rodes

El Port de la Selva

For lunch, make the 30-minute drive up and over the cape to Cadaqués, following the road signposted at the corner of the bay. On the outskirts of the town a signpost marks the road to **Portlligat** one mile (1.6km) to the north. This is the cove Salvador Dalí made his own. Parts of his garden – a camel, a pool, the two eggs representing Dalí and his wife, Gala – are visible on the drive down from the little white *ermita* (hermitage) and though the home he made from two fishermen's cottages is not yet open to the public, it is intriguing to stand before its daubed doors. He picked a beautiful spot beside the uniquely green-and-black painted fishing boats, and it is largely due to him that it has remained unspoiled. The only recent building in the bay is the **Portlligat Hotel**. There is a small charge to spend the day in its well-sited, salt-water swimming pool and lunchtime snacks of set dishes of meat or fish with salad and chips are served on tables set beside it.

Return to **Cadaqués** in the late afternoon to stroll around the cobbled streets of boutiques and pottery shops that lead up to an oversized church. It is a pretty fishing village, Spain's answer to St Tropez, and rather of that same Sixties era: artists and drop-outs still head for its beaches and bars.

The **Casino**, the main town café, is a grand sea-front building with an upstairs art gallery. Behind it is a pretty, tiny theatre and museum, with Dalí's stage design work and wax models of Dalí and Picasso and the old bus that ran from Port de la Selva to Cadaquez. The theatre is one of several venues for music and cinema festivals in summer. Several restaurants have outside tables overlooking the sea. But don't drink if you're driving back inland, either via El Port de la Selva and Llança, or via Roses. Both can be difficult roads. You could head for **Sant Pere de Rodes** and watch the sun come up again.

Dalí's house in Portlligat

3. The Bay of Roses

Aiguamolls bird sanctuary; Greek and Roman remains; the canals of Empúria-brava; boating in the coves of Cap de Creus.

From Cap de Creus in the north to the Montgrí massif in the south, the Bay of Roses is a great sandy sweep 8 miles (13km) long. This eastern edge of the Empordà plain was once covered with a web of lakes and lagoons formed by the Fluvia and Muga rivers, causing the first settlers to live on islands. Today there are still a few inland marshes, turned into a 'little Venice' at Empúria-brava and preserved for wildlife at Aiguamolls.

An early start brings rewards at **Aiguamolls**. The information centre is signposted on the road between Castello d'Empúries and Sant Pere Pescador, and this is the best place to begin exploring some of the 18-square-mile (47km^2) bird sanctuary. Entrance is free and visitors follow the marked trail alongside reed-filled waterways. There should be something new to see among the variety of birds, from nesting storks, green woodpeckers, hoopoes and warblers, to black-winged stilts and waders. Binoculars can be rented from the information centre, which opens at 9am.

After an hour or two here, take the road south, following the signposts to L'Escala, through Sant Pere Pescador, L'Armentera and Montiró, and then turn left on to the Girona–L'Escala road. Just past the second roadside ceramic emporium a turning on the

The Bay of Roses

left to **Sant Martí** is signposted. On reaching the old village wall in about a mile (1.6km), turn right, skirting the buildings and arriving by the beach where there is room to park. Walk up into Sant Martí, a pretty hamlet not much bigger than its pine-shaded square. This is a pleasant place for a coffee or drink. Casa Coll is friendly, and it serves good warm croissants. A tour will take less than 20mins. In the façade of the church are 10th-century tablets commemorating the reconstruction of the building which is on the site of a Greek temple, for this is **Palaeopolis**, where the Phocaean Greeks first settled in Spain.

The 'little Venice' of Empuria-brava

Take the car and continue down the coast road, passing the much larger site of the Neapolis, the Greek new town, and Roman remains. Turn right immediately before the **Ampurias Hotel** to reach the entrance to the site. It is open from 10am–7pm and there is an entrance fee. A 64-page guide is on sale and it is a worthwhile souvenir of one of Spain's most important Roman sites. This is where the Romans, under Scipio, first set foot on the peninsula, in their pursuit of Hannibal. The acres of foundation walls beside the sea are only half of it. Behind the small museum is the Roman part of the town which ends with an impressive south wall.

For a late lunch and lazy afternoon, drive back up past Aiguamolls to the Figueres–Roses road and turn right towards Roses. After 5mins turn right into the **Empúria-brava** complex. This 20-acre (8ha) area of new town, built on canals, is a hive of activity. An information centre immediately on the right on entering the estate is well signposted. Carry on down the central boulevard, taking the second exit at the roundabout, Avinguda Joan Carles. After about a mile (1.6km), just before arriving at the port, the road goes over a bridge. On the far side on the right is CBC **Car Express**. The company is one of several renting out boats by the hour or by the day. (Non-nautical persons can simply take a ferry trip round the canals, which begins on the other side of the bridge.)

Before setting off, visit the nearby **Montserrat supermarket** and fix up a picnic to eat while pottering around these quiet waterways or in one of the pleasant little coves beyond Roses beneath Cap de Creus.

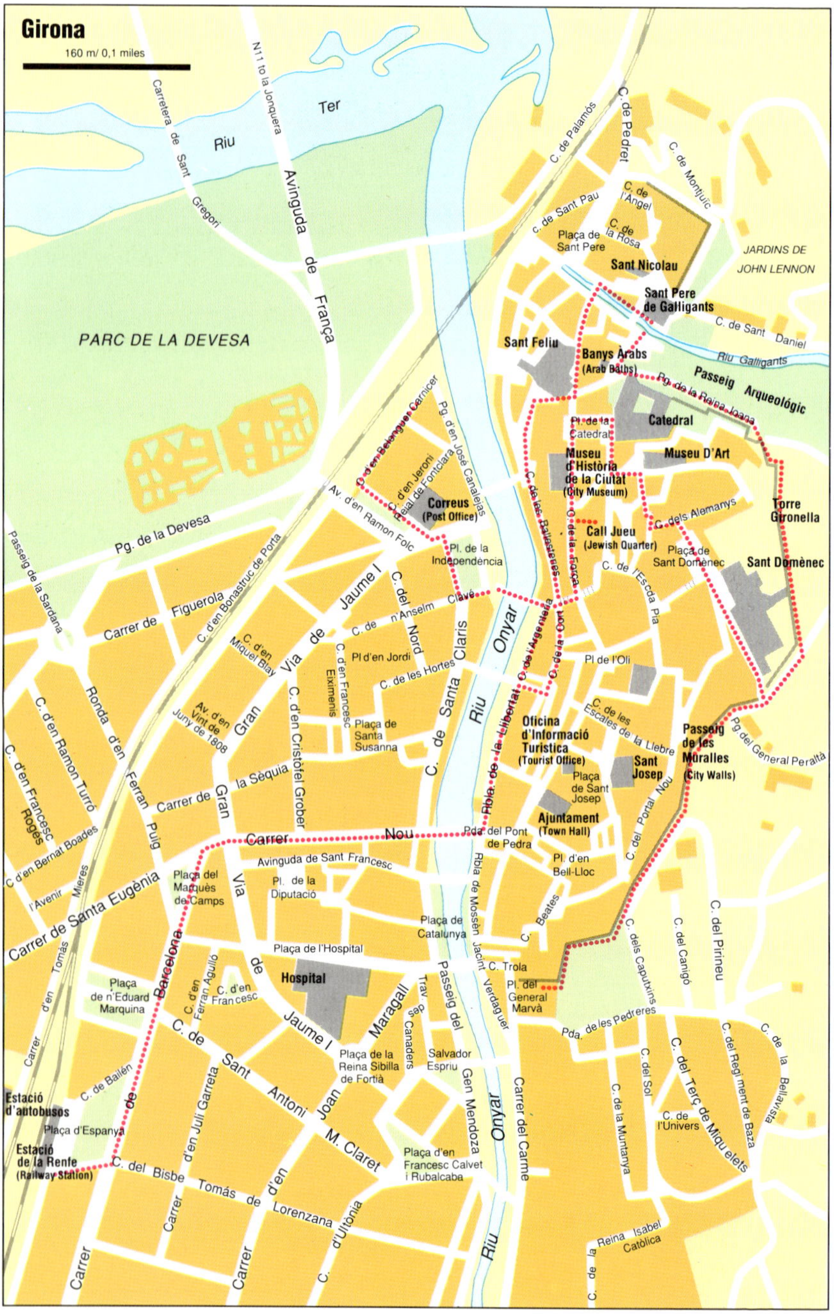
Girona
160 m/ 0,1 miles
Riu Ter
N11 to la Jonquera
Carretera de Sant Gregori
Avinguda de França
PARC DE LA DEVESA
C. de Palamós
C. de Pedret
C. de Montjuïc
C. de l'Àngel
C. de Sant Pau
Plaça de Sant Pere
C. de la Rosa
Sant Nicolau
JARDINS DE JOHN LENNON
Sant Pere de Galligants
C. de Sant Daniel
Riu Galligants
Sant Feliu
Banys Àrabs
(Arab Baths)
Passeig Arqueològic
Pg. de la Reina Joana
Catedral
Pl. de la Catedral
Museu d'Història de la Ciutat
(City Museum)
Museu D'Art
Torre Gironella
C. dels Alemanys
Plaça de Sant Domènec
Sant Domènec
Call Jueu
(Jewish Quarter)
C. de la Força
C. de les Ballesteries
C. de l'Escola Pia
C. d'en Bellmirall
C. d'en Jeroni Real de Fonticlara
Pg. d'en José Canalejas
Correus
(Post Office)
Av. d'en Ramon Folc
Pl. de la Independència
Pg. de la Devesa
Passeig de la Sardana
C. d'en Bonastruc de Porta
Carrer de Figuerola
Gran Via de Jaume I
C. del Nord
C. de n'Anselm Clavé
C. d'en Miquel Blay
C. de Santa Clara
Pl d'en Jordi
C. d'en Francesc Eiximenis
C. de les Hortes
Riu Onyar
C. de l'Argenteria
C. de la Cort Reial
Pl de l'Oli
Rbla. de la Llibertat
Av. d'en Vint de Juny de 1808
Ronda d'en Ferran Puig
C. d'en Ramon Turró
C. d'en Francesc Rogés
C. d'en Cristòfol Grober
Plaça de Santa Susanna
Oficina d'Informació Turística
(Tourist Office)
C. de les Escales de la Llebre
Sant Josep
Plaça de Sant Josep
Passeig de les Muralles
(City Walls)
Pg. del General Peralta
C. del Portal Nou
Ajuntament
(Town Hall)
Carrer de la Sèquia
Carrer Nou
Pda. del Pont de Pedra
C. d'en Bernat Boades
Avinguda de Sant Francesc
Pl. d'en Bell-Lloc
l'Avenir
Mieres
Carrer de Santa Eugènia
Plaça del Marquès de Camps
Pl. de la Diputació
Rbla de Mossèn Jacint Verdaguer
Plaça de Catalunya
C. Beates
C. dels Caputxins
C. del Canigó
C. del Pirineu
Plaça de l'Hospital
Hospital
C. Trola
Pl. del General Marvà
Carrer d'en Tomàs
Plaça de n'Eduard Marquina
C. d'en Ferran Agulló
C. d'en Francesc
Carrer de Barcelona
Trav. des Canaders
Passeig del Gen Mendoza
Pda. de les Pedreres
C. de Sant Antoni
Joan M. Claret
Plaça de la Reina Sibilla de Fortià
Salvador Espriu
C. del Sol
C. del Terç de Miquelets
C. del Regiment de Baza
C. de la Bellavista
C. de l'Univers
C. de Bailèn
Estació d'autobusos
Plaça d'Espanya
Estació de la Renfe
(Railway Station)
C. d'en Juli Garreta
C. de la Muntanya
Carrer del Carme
Plaça d'en Francesc Calvet i Rubalcaba
C. del Bisbe Tomás de Lorenzana
C. d'Ultònia
C. de la Reina Isabel Catòlica
Carrer
Carrer d'en

Girona

4. Provincial Capital

It is something of a scandal that so few people who visit the Costa Brava are acquainted with its capital city, Girona. The old quarter, of cobbled streets, stone steps, alleys, arches and ironwork, is a delight to walk around, its shops are interesting, its restaurants need sampling, its history is visible and absorbing and its museums are brimming with treasures.

There is a daily market near the Plaça de Catalunya and in summer the Saturday market is held in the Devesa park on the north side of town. Museums are closed on Monday. It really needs two or three days to take everything in, but a large amount can be seen with an early start, say around 9am.

The Girona waterfront

If you arrive in Girona by train, turn left out of the station; after a few minutes the road reaches the Plaça Marqués de Camps. Leave the square from the top right-hand corner, crossing as you do, the Gran Via and turn down either the Avinguda de Sant Francesc or Carrer Nou. Halfway down is Can Batlle, fronting both streets, designed by the Girona *Modernista* architect Rafael Masó in 1910 and topped by sunny yellow owls. The end of these roads leads over the Pont de Pedra, and left into the Rambla de la Llibertat.

If coming by car, the best place to park is on the north side of town beneath the raised railway beside the N-II through-road, opposite the Devesa park. From there head towards the river, through the Plaça de la Independència, and its statue to the defenders of the city during the terrible siege in the Napoleonic wars.

One of the three footbridges crossing the river from here is an iron mesh cage built by the French Eiffel company. These all lead into the old city and the Rambla with its *Modernista* shop fronts, overhanging balconies, shady plane trees and outdoor café tables.

Bookshops full of creaking shelves are worth a browse, as is the philatelist, the hardware shop, the boutiques and toy shops.

At the back of the Rambla are the **Voltes**, the arcaded area of old shops, *patisseries*, grocers and art galleries. From here walk up the Carrer de la Força, the old Roman *Via Augusta*, a surprisingly narrow street for the grand route from Gaul (and therefore Rome) to the rest of Spain: no more than half a dozen legionaries could have marched abreast. On the right is the Carrer de Sant Lorenç, a steep alley which leads to the **Isaac el Cec Centre**, the newly opened Jewish quarter. It is worth a visit, and a brief rest in its courtyard before continuing: there are still two important museums to be visited before they close for lunch at 1pm.

The monastery of Sant Domenéc

Continue up Carrrer de la Força to the baroque **cathedral square**. Opposite is the 18th-century Casa Pastors, now the provincial courts of justice. On the right is the 16th-century Gothic almshouse, now housing the College of Architects. On the left is the Portal de Sobreportes, the north gate of the Roman town. At its base are huge stones from the original Iberian settlement. Above it is the Virgin of Good Death, who in later centuries looked down on the condemned who were taken from the city through this gate to be executed.

Climb the 90 steps up to the elegant **cathedral**, built between the 14th and 18th centuries. Inside is Guillermo Bofill's exceptional nave, the widest outside St Peter's in Rome. An unusual canopy hangs over the altar and behind it is a copy of an alabaster chair, supposedly built for Charlemagne who almost certainly never came to sit in it. To the left is the **cathedral museum**, which must be visited to see such treasures as the beautifully illustrated 10th-century *Beatus*, and the stunning 11th-century *Tapestry of the Creation*. The museum leads into the cloister of the older, Romanesque church, over which the cathedral was built. Beside the museum in the Plaça dels Apóstols is the **Museu d'Art**, the city's other essential place to visit. Situated in the former Bishop's Palace, it has a wonderful collection of paintings, mainly from the Romanesque and Gothic periods, which once brightened the province's church interiors, as well as some fine art from the 19th and 20th centuries.

Lunch in the **Hostalet del Call** restaurant off the Plaça dels Lledoners to the right of the museum: the food is imaginative and plentiful. Afterwards walk the meal off along the city walls, reached by going back up the town towards the Monastery of **Sant Domènec**. This is the university area, which is undergoing

La Terra café in Girona

expansion. Behind the monastery a large breech in the old walls allows them to be scaled and explored in both directions. The section to the south is a 20-minute walk leading down towards the River Onyar and the Plaça de Catalunya. To the left, it skirts the back of the city, offering excellent views of the spires and rooftops. This section ends behind the cathedral at the start of the Passeig Arqueològic and near the **Arab Baths**. By now it should be after 4.30pm, so the baths will be open for an afternoon visit. Built in the 13th century, they show how much the architecture of the Moors was appreciated long after they had gone. The cold room, centred on an octagonal lantern with Romanesque pillars, is perfect.

Just below the Arab Baths is another piece of perfection: **Sant Pere de Galligants**, built in the most sophisticated Romanesque style. A former Benedictine monastery, it has been deconsecrated, and it now houses the main provincial archaeological collection, both in its aisles and in upstairs rooms. In the cloisters are *stelles*, gravestones from the Jewish burial ground above the city, Montjuïc.

About 50 yards (46m) back up from the building a street leads over the Galligants (cock crow) stream and up the Pujada del Rei Martí. At ankle level on either side of this street are lintels and tops of arches, the remains of the buildings' ground floors, sunk in centuries of persistent flooding of the Onyar and Ter. At the top of the street on the right is **Sant Feliu**, the city's main church. It is Gothic and rather gloomy but there are a number of interesting items including Roman sarcophagi and memorials to the heroes and heroines of the 1809 siege, and to several Counts of Barcelona.

Return to the Rambla by following the Pujada de Sant Feliu, the road sloping down beside the church, to narrow **Les Ballesteries** with its delightful little shops and cafés. You should reach the Rambla in time for the evening *passejada* or stroll, and at a café table in the Rambla you can watch the whole Girona world walk by.

5. The Medes Islands

From L'Estartit, spend the morning cruising round the Medes Islands in a glass-bottomed boat. In the afternoon explore L'Estartit by bike. Take swimming costumes if it's hot.

L'Estartit, 25 miles (40km) east of Girona is a cheery, modern resort with a sandy beach and active port. It lies beneath the limestone massif of Montgrí which ends in a dramatic cliff overlooking the six Medes islands a mile (1.6km) out to sea. Around them Spain's first marine conservation area has been established, with the result that fish and coral are growing large again and diving is safe and popular. Just inland is Torroella de Montgrí, an unspoilt, historic town.

On arrival at **L'Estartit**, follow the main road to the right down the Passeig Marítim (seafront) and park as near the port as possible. Booths sell tickets for trips round the islands. They are all similar, although not all boats are small enough to enter the caves (small boats may not be best in a swelling sea). Shorter trips circumnavigate the former pirates' islands, now uninhabited except for gulls, guillemots and shags. The longer trip is however preferable. It continues up under the barren Montgrí cliffs towards L'Escala, taking about an hour with occasional stops to peer down at the marine life through the boat's glass bottom.

To explore the town, rent out a bike. **Velo Beach** at 60 Passeig Marítim, is one of several places hiring out all sorts of transport from mopeds to four-person bicycles. An hour is long enough on these unwieldy machines. Before you leave, children may enjoy the go-karts at the amusement parks found on the edge of town.

To restore belief that this is actually Spain, return on the only road inland to **Torroella de Montgrí**, a solid, baronial town and once an important port at the mouth of the Ter. Follow the main road as it loops around the town and take the left turn signposted to the town centre. Park in front of the church and walk through the gateway to the right, beside the walled garden of a large private house which the Girona *Modernista* architect, Rafael Masó, restored at the beginning of this century. The entrance to the **church** is on the far side. It is a severe, Gothic building, but its accoustics are good enough to attract international musicians.

The tree-lined Passeig de l'Església leads to the attractive Plaça de la Vila. Continue down the Carrer Major directly opposite to reach the small local **museum** (11am–2pm, 6–9pm, free) which explains some of the geography, prehistory, flora and fauna of the Medes Islands, the Montgrí massif and the lowlands of the River Ter, on which the town once stood. Return to the square for a drink outside the café. On the left is a typically elaborate sundial. Opposite is a plaque commemorating the fact that the *sardana* was first danced here in its present form in 1844. If it is getting late, there are several little *fondes* (restaurants) in the town.

6. Ullastret and La Bisbal

This is a tour of ancient and medieval Catalonia beginning at the largest site of Iberian remains in the region and continuing to two nearby medieval villages for lunch. Finally there is a shopping trip to the principal ceramic town, La Bisbal.

Ullastret is often overlooked, perhaps because it is slightly off the beaten track, perhaps because the Iberians don't sound as exciting as the Ancient Greeks or Romans. But it is well worth a visit (closed Monday and each lunchtime from 1–4pm). Signposted on

Ceramicist's wares in La Bisbal

the left after passing through La Bisbal, 22 miles (35.4km) east of Girona on the C255, Ullastret is approached via a capacious car park. There is a small entrance fee which includes access to a good museum. The grounds are rather like a pleasant park, well planted with trees among the ruins of this fortified town which flourished from the 6th to 2nd centuries BC, at which time it was eclipsed by nearby Empúries.

Ullastret sits on a hill, which was once an isthmus, and from outside the museum building there is an excellent view over the surrounding plains from which the River Daró collects its water. It is easy to imagine this as a lake, which is what it was when Ullastret was fully occupied, and has been again in living memory, particularly after heavy rains. (A few fields of rice, formerly an important crop to the area, are still cultivated and sold 8 miles/13km away at the river's mouth.)

From Ullastret go back towards La Bisbal, turning left to **Peratallada** after about a mile (1.6km). Don't enter Peratallada immediately, but follow the road round until reaching a Romanesque church on the left, with an unusual bell wall. If it is open, have a look around this double-naved curiosity. Peratallada's north gate is nearby, approached over a moat cut into the rock, which almost surrounds the town. Nothing is hard to find in the cobbled lanes: the restaurants, glass, ceramic and antique shops, and the noble house at the centre. This now contains a restaurant, but is otherwise closed to the public, which is a pity, because it has an interesting interior, from typical carved beds to an impressive kitchen.

Good restaurants for lunch are Bonay, El Patí, and Can Nau (closed Wednesday). Or have a snack in the Can Vell in the Plaça del Castell. In the afternoon continue along the same road, turning up left after a few minutes to **Sant Julià de Boada**. This little

Baix Empordà from Ullastret

10th-century church, long used for cattle, has a horseshoe entrance arch in the Mozarabic style, a legacy from the Moors.

At the junction at the end of the road, turn right to **Pals** and use the large parking area at the foot of the town. Dominated by a round clock tower and small transitional church, this arrangement of honey-coloured stones is larger than Peratallada, which seceded from it in 1501. But its history is less glorious than its sturdy streets suggest. It never had a large population, and as a result was not attractive to kings, counts and other landlords who found little to tax. It is the most handsome of the province's medieval towns, and an hour or two can be lost in the lanes that wander beneath arches, and up to the mirador of **El Pedró** with its broad view of the neat farmlands of the lower Empordà. There is a small museum near the church and local ceramicists exhibit their wares.

The main ceramic town of the province is **La Bisbal**: right and right again out of the town. Dozens of shops line the main through road, their pots and tiles spilling brightly on to the pavement. No two shops are the same and it is worth visiting as many as possible before buying, as styles and prices vary. Afterwards cross the bridge over the Daró and at the café beneath the neo-classical colonnade order a drink of thick, creamy *xocolata*.

Cap Sa Sal

7. The Coves of Begur

The unspoiled beaches of the 'wild, rugged coast' which gave the Costa Brava its name.

The 40-minute twisting drive from Sant Feliu to Tossa is the classic Costa Brava corniche. But an easier route to the coves, cliffs and little sandy bays which typify the coast begins further north at **Begur**, 25 miles (40km) due east of Girona. From here roads run like rivulets down into the bays: Sa Riera, Aiguafreda, Sa Tuna, Fornells, Aiguablava, Aiguaxelida, Tamariu. None are spoilt with high-rise hotels, though the hills that surround them are increasingly urbanised with weekend villas.

Toss a coin to choose a beach for the day. Each has yellow sand surrounding pine-clad cliffs overlooking clear blue water. **Aiguafreda** and **Aiguaxelida** are the smallest bays, with barely a café on the beach. **Sa Riera** and **Sa Tuna** manage small hotels and restaurants, where the classic Mediterranean lunch of grilled sardines and salad should be eaten, washed down with cold pink (*rosat*) wine.

Just north of Aiguafreda, at **Cap Sa Sal**, is an extraordinary apartment complex quite out of keeping with the small fishing-village atmosphere of the other places. Set high on a bluff, it has

The pine-clad hills and the bay at Aiguablava

fabulous views and was built in the 1950s as the last word in luxury. Franco's daughter regularly stayed here and an internal lift went down to the beach where a liveried flunky would fetch guests' boats. There are still rooms to let at Apartamentos Aiguafreda: the Rosa suite is as much as a five-star Barcelona hotel.

To get back to reality, the last of these resorts is **Tamariu**, officially part of Palafrugell rather than Begur, but reached easily from either town. It is a lovely old-fashioned spot, long popular with the English. In the 1920s Lord Islington, a Tory minister, built a villa inland and was the first tourist to stay here in winter. Times have changed and the fishermen's homes have been given over to tourist apartments, but a timeless charm remains. White-jacketed waiters serve pots of tea at the respectable **Tamariu Hotel**. Finally, at the heart of these coves, between Tamariu and Cap de Begur, lie the twin bays of **Fornells** and **Aiguablava**. This is where in 1911, at the family home of a parliamentarian, a journalist named Ferran Agulló made a speech in which he termed this wild, rugged coast, the *costa brava* for the first time.

Xiquet Sabater, the parliamentarian's son, has since turned the family home into one of the most sought after hotels on the coast. The **Aiguablava** at Fornells, unimposing, discreet and choosy about who its guests are (Sabater mixes them to ensure there are never too many of one nationality), is a fine place for an evening meal. If it is full, try the state-run **parador** on the promontory opposite. This modern building is not very appealing to look at, but it is well situated and has an excellent reputation for food.

8. A Night Out in La Platja d'Aro

Early-evening shopping; seafront stroll; dinner, bars and discos.

The nightlife of the coast is not the sole preserve of tourists. Young people from all over Girona as well as Barcelona head for the resorts at weekends, mainly to Lloret de Mar and **La Platja d'Aro**, which is a new invention. Three miles (5km) from the real town of Castell d'Aro, it is a sandy beach (*platja*) along which hotels have been lined. It is a clean, modern, tidy place which out of season is host to sober parties of ageing Europeans and conferring businessmen who like their comfort. Food in the hotels is generally good.

La Platja d'Aro does, however, have more discos and nightclubs than anywhere else on the coast, and in August it is packed. Tourists are shoulder to shoulder on the pavements and the main through road, Carretera de Sant Feliu de Guíxols, is so busy that subways have been built so people can cross it.

Carretera de Sant Feliu de Guíxols

There is no point in going to a disco until midnight. Start with an early-evening shop along the main road where smart cars will be cruising and style watchers will be sitting outside places such as Montbar, the Max Pub or Harry's Bar, drinking rash cocktails like Blue Sky or Green Peace or even Siborsky, a straight mix of vodka and Calvados. The shops (open until around 11pm) are devoted mostly to clothes. Large stores such as Montserrat and Marbill, on the corner of La Paz, specialise in leather, and there are spacious shoe and bag shops, too. Top Barcelona designer clothes are on the racks and an Italian shirt at Bruto's can cost a day's wage. In the lanes up behind La Paz there are basketwork shops, jewellers and art galleries as well as boutiques.

Before dinner, have a stroll on the seafront, the **Passeig Marítim**, which runs parallel to the main street. Take a *tisana* cocktail at one of the smart bars (most belong to hotels). Or walk up the Carrer de l'Església to the jolly Don Quixote, a lively *bar tipico* where prices are kept down. They serve *pinchos* here, small kebabs of spiced meat. The evening could progress on small platters of *tapes* such as these, moving on perhaps to Meson Canaletes, in the Centre Canaletes, which has a good choice, or El Cid in Carrer Pau, which serves plates of cold meats, to go with *tancs* of beer.

For a proper meal, walk northwards (towards Palamós), and just as the bright lights seem to fade, they come on again, on the right, as the road goes uphill, where there are two extremely good restau-

rants: the **Trebol**, for meat eaters, and the **Xaco**, which has a wide selection of fresh fish. In between, for the undecided, **La Ostra** serves *tapes*. Afterwards, to get into the mood for the evening, head right to the other end of the town, to the corner of **Avinguda de Madrid**. At the Llevant on the left have a game of bowls (ticket price includes shoes) or shoot some pool. Opposite is Magic Park, where a ghost train is among the indoor amusements. Upstairs, roller disco dancers will have begun to bop.

After midnight, things start to get lively. Huge screens in the bars show cable TV and videos, and a whole wall on the side of the **Galerias Neptune** becomes a picture show. 'Public relations' people from the discos tout for business, offering free tickets to respectable looking customers. Entry may be free (if not, expect to pay about 2,000 pesetas), but drinks inside are obligatory. They can range from around 500 pesetas for a Coke or a beer. There is live music at Chaplin's, Decada and the Piano Bar. Kamel and the Malibu are for the smart set. Marius has a good friendly atmosphere and BB's is a popular place for serious drinking and dancing.

Towards the end of the evening, about 4am, the 'in' crowd heads for **Maddox**, several bars and dance floors in the hotel of the same name in Avinguda Cavall Bernat at the north end of the Passeig Marítim. Come dawn, one or two revellers will have failed to keep out of the swimming pool. Those who do not manage to get in are free to cool off in the sea.

Blanes

9. Plants in Profusion

Blanes has one of Spain's best botanic gardens; a visit here can be combined with a trip to the flower market of Mataró.

In high season, this excursion should be undertaken with a stout heart: Blanes is a busy package-holiday resort, and beyond it, where the Costa Maresme begins, the N-II is an unpleasant highway which hurtles alongside the sea. It is necessary to use this road to reach the **Mercat de Flor i Planta Ornamental de Catalunya** flower market at Vilassar de Mar. The market is only open to the public from 3–6pm on Monday, Tuesday and Wednesday. Take swimming things for a cooling dip in the sea.

Blanes, 25 miles (40km) south of Girona, is the southernmost resort in the Costa Brava. It was once a pretty little fishing village. Now high-rises spread along its sandy beach. The botanic gardens are at the top of the town, behind the port. The road to the gardens is narrow and the parking poor, so it is best to catch one of the buses which regularly go up to them from the port.

Along with an entrance ticket, visitors are given a leaflet briefly describing the gardens, which were established at the turn of the

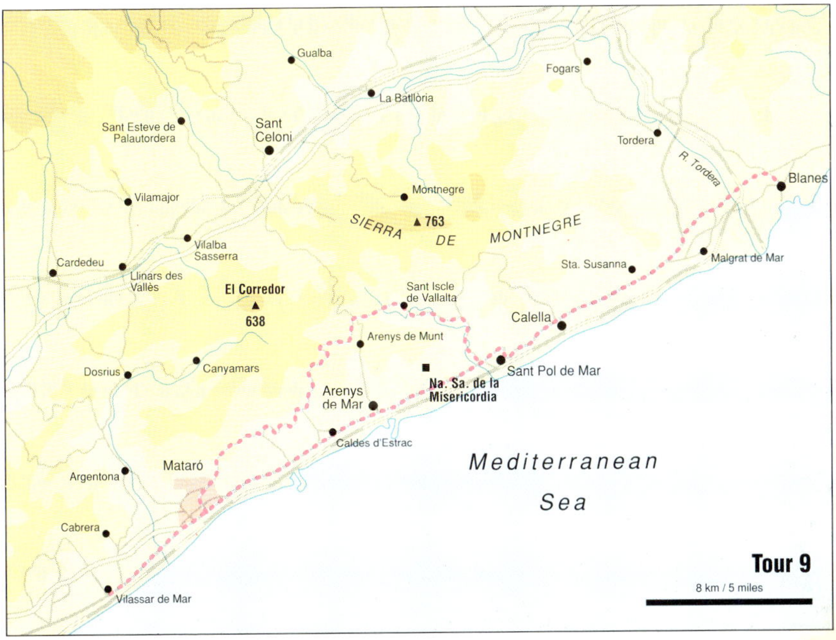

century by a German businessman, Karl Faust, and are now maintained by The International Station of Mediterranean Biology, a centre of education and research. Beautifully situated overlooking the sea, they are a pleasure to wander round discovering plants which have proliferated on the coast, many of which were imported in the last century from South America (eg the century plant, or agave) and South Africa (the hottentot fig, pictured right).

Afterwards head south to Malgrat where the N-II's coastal stretch begins. Crossing the River Tordera, which forms the boundary between Girona and Barcelona provinces, and between the Costa Brava and the Costa Maresme, allotments and nurseries begin to appear. After 8 miles (13km), at Sant Pol, turn inland and escape to the hills for lunch. This road, through Sant Cebrià and Sant Iscle de Vallalta, arrives after another 8 miles (13km) at **Arenys de Munt**. This is a typical Catalan small town, centred on a shady *rambla,* or dried-up river bed, and a good inexpensive set-menu meal can be eaten at the Caliu restaurant. This is where the locals go, so you can be assured of good food.

Continue on the inland road 12 miles (19.3km) to **Mataró** and there join the motorway again. Keep a good lookout for the **flower market**. It is a modern warehouse, set back a little from the road on the right, 4 miles (6.4km) south of Mataró. Inside are a variety of healthy and colourful plants for sale to the trade – this is where the flower sellers of Barcelona's famous Rambla come to buy. The red rose of St George is Catalonia's national flower, but carnations are more numerous, and they form large swaths of the flower

Arenys de Munt

carpets which coat the pavements of Arbúcies and Figueres during the feast of Corpus Christi.

To end the day, take a break to cool off and have a drink at **Caldes d'Estrac** between Mataró and Arenys de Mar (the former fishing village of Arenys de Munt). This little resort has an elegant air, pleasant little sandy beaches and a shady bar in the square.

MONTSENY

10. From the Sea to the Mountains

A scenic mountain drive with a stop at Breda, taking in ceramics, crafts, rustic restaurants and mountain footpaths along the way.

Montseny provides a natural border between the provinces of Girona and Barcelona. This imposing mountain range is easy to pick out from a distance: its long line of blunt fingers atop the verdant hills, rising above 4,000ft (1,219m). Its vegetation mixes cork oaks

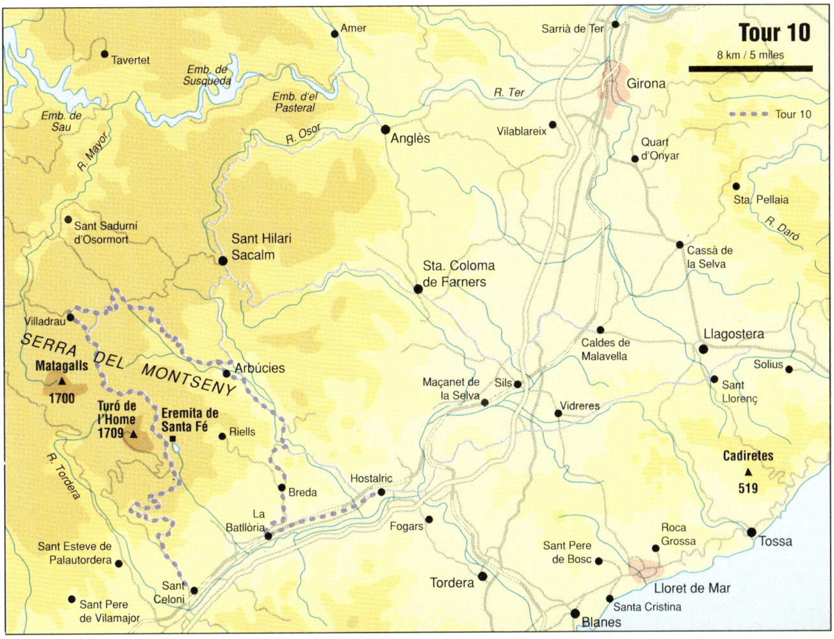

Outside fortified Hostalric

with Scots pine, beech with maple and chestnut. Its most distinguished peak is the Turó de l'Home and there is a centre for walking is nearby at Santa Fe. The quickest way up to it is from the town of Sant Celoni, 15 miles (24km) to the south on the C251 (exit 11 on the motorway). A barrier closes the road off to traffic if there is snow.

For a day of greater variety, there is an optional, stunning 45-mile (72.4-km) loop of a drive to be made via Breda and the Guilleries to the north. This wonderful scenic mountain route, passing through Arbúcies and Viladrau, gives a panorama of Montseny and such a feeling of extreme remoteness that on reaching Viladrau the traveller is left wondering how such a village came to be built here at all. Start out on this tour at around 11am to catch the museum at Arbúcies and to make the lunch stop.

Taking either the C251 or exit 10 on the motorway, skirt around the edge of Hostalric and then continue on 3 miles (5km) south to Breda. (The fortifications of Hostalric are best appreciated from the outside. Inside, the town is rather cramped and claustrophobic and

Viladrau, in the mountains of Montseny

Arbúcies

apart from the castle, which is now a restaurant, there is not that much to see.) Stop in **Breda** where the church of Sant Salvador has an interesting five-storey Romanesque tower. There are also good-value ceramic shops to be found here: this is the best centre for picking up ordinary earthenware cooking and garden pots, and the ceramicists are located on the main road alongside plant and flower shops.

Continue on for 8 miles (13km) up to **Arbúcies**, known as 'the garden of the Guilleries'. It is not really much more than a one-street town, but it is worth making a stop here. In the main road, Carrer Camprodón, are good *pastisseries*. Notable and delicious local specialities include *pa de pessic*, a fennel-flavoured sponge cake, and *delícies de Montseny,* which are honey macaroons. Those with a sophisticated sweet tooth will want to sample these delicacies. Wander up through the main square to the **museum** (daily, 12–2pm; 5–7pm). This is another of the province's small triumphs. It is extremely well laid out and gives an insight into the life of the town, and its crafts and industries, principally coach building. (Evidence of the importance of this particular industry can be seen in the large sheds found to the west of the town, on the road to Viladrau; 40 per cent of the town's working population is employed here.)

For lunch take the road signposted to Vic, past the Parc El Mong. After about one mile (1.6km) on the left is **Les Pipes**, a delightful old restaurant of rickety wood tables and floors situated by a spring and approached over a small stone bridge. Food is mostly grilled, and there is a trout tank at the back from which you can select your dinner.

Return to Arbúcies and take the slow, winding road leading to **Viladrau**, 12 miles (19.3km) west. Stop for a stretch in this tranquil alpine village, and perhaps try a coffee in one of its cafés or small hotels. Afterwards head back up the same road and take the turn-off to Turó de l'Home and Santa Fe. After 10 miles (16km) you will find a large restaurant with a parking area on the left. Stop here, put on your hiking boots, and walk along any of the recommended mountain paths. Return by driving the easy 15-mile (24-km) route down to Sant Celoni.

Vic

11. Cathedral Town

Cathedral, belfry and frescoes; Romanesque treasures in the episcopal museum; good and unpretentious food; tea with a view.

This cathedral and market town lies in the Plain of Vic (see map on page 53), a hinterland of climatic extremes: roasting in summer and chilly in winter. It is a stoical, conservative place, which allows only a restrained flourish of *Noucentisme*, the more classical style which followed *Modernisme*. It is easiest to reach from the south, via Granollers just north of Barcelona, on the N152. Crossing over from Girona via Angles or from Santa Coloma de Farners is shorter in distance, but takes longer because of the winding, mountainous roads. Tuesday and Saturday, market days, are the best times to go, when a visit to the museum and cathedral can relieve the shopping. The **old quarter** (*casc antic*) is in the middle of the town surrounded by wide roads (*rambles*).

On market day the attraction is obviously the stalls in the large **Plaça Major**. There are kitchen gadgets, pots, pans, clothes, shoes, linen, flowers, as well as piles of vegetables, cheeses and cold meats. Vic is well-known for its sausages (*embotits*, especially the sticks of salami-like meats, *fuets*). At the back of the square is an information office and beside it to the right a lane leads to the **cathedral** and

Vic market in the Plaça Major

museum. The cathedral's façade is not particularly attractive, nor does it have a grand approach; in fact its entrance is a small door on its north side beside the magnificent Romanesque belfry, a reminder of its grandeur under Abbot Oliba. The interior is quite unexpected. The walls, divided by five gilded pillars, are entirely painted with pale sepia figures and scenes, relieved by swaths of red where garments and cloth are draped, giving a grand theatrical effect. The paintings, by Josep Maria Sert (1874–1945), were his second attempt, the first having been destroyed in the Civil War.

The **episcopal museum** opposite the cathedral entrance, though small, must not be overlooked. Situated above the cathedral cloisters, its main attractions are the bright Romanesque altar fronts, especially from La Seu d'Urgell, and statuary. Upstairs are ceramics, textiles and ironwork, and memorabilia of Jacint Verdaguer (1845–1902), the poet-priest born in Folgueroles, who led the 19th-century revival of the Catalan language.

Susqueda reservoir

Carrer Cloquer, between the cathedral and the museum, leads to an uninspiring mock-Roman temple beside the remains of a Romanesque church and the palace of the Montcada family. Turn left down **Carrer de Cardona** and join the throngs in the shopping lanes that lead back to the main square. This is where to find refreshment, in the busy cafés and *tapes* bars. For a late, leisurely lunch, leave Vic around 1pm, as everything begins to close, taking the C153 towards Olot, on the east side of the town. After 3 miles (5km) follow the signposted road to the Vic Parador. After just over one mile (1.6km) into this hilly countryside another signpost points to **Fusimanya**. This hamlet consists mainly of a restaurant, **The Fusimanya**, an unpretentious, popular single-storey building. The cold meat first course is served like a French cheeseboard and left on the table. Grilled meats include whole rabbit with *allioli* (garlic). Ask for a brandy or whisky at the end of the meal and the bottle will be left on the table.

To cool off afterwards, there is a nearby swimming pool. Then make further into the hills, to the **Vic Parador**. These state-run hotels are generally housed in old castles or manorial homes, but this one was purpose-built in the 1940s. Its attraction is its site. The red cliffs before it in the distance descend into the deep blue Susqueda reservoir like a mini Grand Canyon. Take in the view with tea on the terrace. These hotels are renowned for their cuisine, always based on local dishes. But perhaps Fusimanya will have put paid to any ambitions for a gourmet evening here.

RIPOLL

12. Cradle of Catalonia

The region's best-preserved Romanesque carvings, the burial place of the Counts of Barcelona and an excellent museum of rural life and local history.

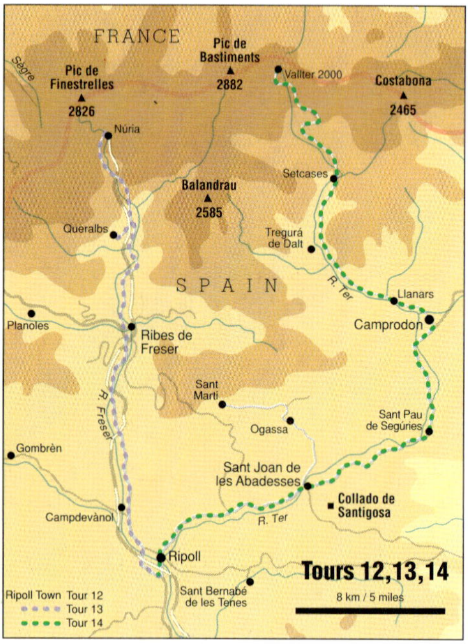

It takes around two hours to get to Ripoll from the coast, but the rewards are great, particularly if combined with a visit to the sister monastery of Sant Joan de les Abadesses.

To see the monastery and the museum at Ripoll, which closes at 1pm, the day needs a reasonably early start. The town is on the confluence of the Ter and the Freser rivers, 55 miles (88.5km) northwest of Girona. The c150 from Olot winds steeply up to around 4,275ft (1,303m) before dropping down to the town in its deep valley.

The monastery church of **Santa Maria** has the most beautiful of all Romanesque carvings on its porch wall, which is protected by glass. Scenes from the Old and New Testaments are described and their characters portrayed along its whole length. It helps to understand that this was once one of the greatest seats of learning in Christendom, particularly under the powerful Abbot Oliba who, in the early 11th century, brought the monastery to academic excellence. Most of the early Counts of Barcelona were buried here, including Guifré el Pilós (Wilfred the Hairy), founder of Catalonia. Unfortunately the ravages of man have not left the rest of the church with much to offer: burnt down during the dissolution of the monasteries in 1835, the whole building was re-erected in 1883. A single tomb of a Count, Berenguer III (who died in 1131), remains. Fortunately the adjoining cloister is intact and

The monastery church of Santa Maria

delightful: the capitals on the lower tier of pillars are carved with inventive figures. Summer concerts take place here when the opera singer Monserrat Caballé sometimes performs.

Next to Santa Maria, in the former church of Sant Pere, is the excellent **ethnographic museum** (entrance fee) which is well worth visiting. It displays artefacts from domestic life in the town, from the shepherds who were once numerous in the mountains, firearms on which the town once prospered, and the *farga catalana*, a method of smelting ore perfected here in the 12th century and used all over the world up to the 20th century. For lunch, leave town on the C153 Sant Joan de les Abadesses road, stopping just outside Ripoll at the great **junk emporium** on the right, where a 20-minute browse among mule collars, marble sinks, furniture, prints and children's pedal cars may be rewarding as well as instructive. Nothing is priced; bartering is essential.

Sant Joan is 6 miles (9.6km) east along the Ter valley, but just before the right turn beside the Gothic bridge into the town, there is a turning to the left, signposted to **Ogassa**. This is the place to go for lunch. It is a former mining village 5 miles (8km) up a cul-de-sac. Park the car and stroll up to the Font Ferro, the fountain with iron-red water. There are two restaurants, the **Can Costa** and the **Can-Tal-Lara**, which is run by the mayor, Ramon Tubert, a local character with a Charlie Chaplin moustache who usually

The waterfront at Ripoll

The monastery of Sant Joan de les Abadesses

wears a traditional Catalan red *barretina*. His restaurant is decked out to look like a mine, and anyone whose Spanish is up to it can hear tales of the lawless times when guns ruled the town, and when miners were rich and respected.

After lunch return to **Sant Joan**, parking in the main car park area behind the monastery. It is a small, unpretentious town. The entrance fee to the monastery allows admittance to a small ecclesiastical museum. Visitors are given a brief descriptive guide in their own language. The **monastery church**, reached through an elegant cloister, is solidly, typically Romanesque. It is cool and beautifully proportioned inside and has a singular attraction: a 12th-century carved and painted wood calvary (one of the crucified thieves was burnt in the Civil War and has been replaced). A bread wafer, inserted in Christ's forehead when it was made, was rediscovered, still intact, earlier this century.

Shop front in Sant Joan de les Abadesses

13. Zip up to Núria

By car to Ribes de Freser, a typical Pyrenean village, then by train to Queralbs and Núria. This spectacular rail journey goes to the top of the Pyrenees, to the sanctuary of Núria at the head of a valley which cannot be reached by car.

This journey starts from Ripoll with a drive along the River Freser to Ribes de Freser. Here we take the train to the pretty mountain village, Queralbs, where Jordi Pujol, president of Catalonia, spends a few weeks in August when it can be busy. Finally we reach Núria where there is a good hour or two's walking with refreshments at the end. In winter this is a ski resort, which uses the turbulent, mist-swirling slopes of Puigmal (7,550ft/2,909m).

The peaceful sanctuary of Núria

Heading north out of Ripoll, our first stop is at the mountain-fresh little town of **Ribes de Freser**, 6 miles (9.6km) north of Ripoll. There is a one-way system through the town. Park where possible. Sunday is market day, when a dozen or so stalls are set up by the river which the town has largely turned its back on: harsh winters have not encouraged the townspeople to put up balconies or verandas looking out over its views. It has several hotels favoured by walkers but it is not particularly a tourist town. It is pleasant just to walk around, to buy bread and hams. The tourist office in the little square beside the church has good walking maps as well as all the necessary information on the area.

From Ribes the **Cremallera**, or Zip train, a rack-and-pinion two-carriage vehicle, goes up to the sanctuary of Núria. It runs every hour or so and is a magnificent scenic journey. It is best, however, not to take the train from here, but to drive up to the first stop, Queralbs, which is as far as the road goes. **Queralbs** is a real Pyrenean mountain village, where cows spatter the narrow lanes, and heavy slates and wood balconies, overhung with flowers, reflect the climate of harsh winters and bright summers. Head for the 10th-century church of **Sant Jaume** at the top of the village. This is a beautiful and unusual building, with a porch of six arches and carved beams. There are a couple of restaurants and a bar where it is worth dropping in for a drink: the best view of the valley is from its toilet window.

Pastoral, Pyrenean Núria

Take the 15-minute train ride from Queralbs to **Núria**, along a precipitous track high above the rock-strewn Freser, past cascading waterfalls, past the treeline, beneath circling birds of prey. In 1967 the Virgin of Núria was made a patron saint of shepherds who have used sanctuaries on this site for 800 years. But the flocks have declined. Now the head of the valley is dominated by a 19th-century **sanctuary**, a large, institutional-looking place which does not have a chance to be overpowering: the surrounding hills are far too majestic. The sanctuary has a hotel, with a large restaurant, and a café. The church can be visited, but it was built at the same time as the sanctuary and holds no great rewards.

In front of the sanctuary is a lake where boats are for hire, where cattle graze and where, in winter, ice-skating takes place. The greatest pleasure is just to take off for the hills, breathe the thin fresh air and feel miles away from the bustle of the coast: it is hard to imagine it is barely two hours away.

Sant Jaume, Queralbs

NOTES

NOTES

14. To the Top of the Ter

A trip to the high peaks of the Pyrenees, in search of local food and flower-filled alpine meadows.

Camprodon

A trip to the top of the Pyrenees, even in summer, can give an idea of the skiing facilities available in January and February. The resort of Vallter 2000 is no great distance from the coast and on a clear day the Bay of Roses is visible from its summits. For preference, take a picnic, though there is no shortage of good eating places, particularly in the pretty mountain village of Setcases. The journey begins at Camprodon, 45mins from Olot either via the C153 and the Val de Bianya, or via the C151 and Sant Joan de les Abadesses (see Tour 12: *Cradle of Catalonia*). An extra sweatshirt may be advisable as the heights are chilly.

Camprodon, on the confluence of the Ter and Ritort, is a small town easily explored. It has two main shopping streets, three squares and the affluent look of a border town, which it virtually is, as there is no town at the Coll d'Ares pass into France, 11 miles (17.7km) away. Park at the top of the town by the 11th-century monastery of Sant Pere, which is only open for special events. In the main street, **Carrer Valencia**, leading off the monastery square, the best local produce is evident. In unnamed shops unlabelled cheese wheels, *foie gras* and round *bulls* (black or white sausage) are piled, alongside rich pastries from shops such as Antigua Casa Sala which sell pine-covered confections shaped like pigs and deer.

Near the ski resort of Vallter 2000

At the end of this street turn left into **Carrer de Isaac Albèniz** (the composer was born here in 1860) to the Forn Sant Roc patisserie and Cal Xec, which cures its own *bulls* and has a choice of long, thin salamis (*fuets*). On reaching the river, the road passes a typical local Gothic bridge before arriving at the Plaça d'Espanya, where the menu of the **Núria Restaurant** should be borne in mind (trout from the River Núria, partridge hunter-style).

Camprodon's shops provide all that is necessary for a picnic,

The Forn Sant Roc patisserie

though the next village, **Setcases**, 15 minutes away, also has good local produce. The road to it leads from the top of Carrer de Isaac Albèniz and is clearly marked. It follows the bubbling Ter north-west, first to **Llanars**, where a quick stop must be made to visit the pretty rose-covered Romanesque church. If it is open, be sure to see the Gothic altar front, now behind glass in the south transept.

Setcases ('seven houses') is a real rural mountain village, smelling of cows and running with dogs. Park down by the river and stroll around. Restaurants and small hotels have grown with the skiing, and their dishes are always both imaginative and hearty. Local cheese is sold in the two village shops and farmhouse bread (*pa de pessic*) is a solid accompaniment.

This is the last village before the Pyrenees's summits. Continue along the road, which goes through the bottom of the village, and head for the hills, following the Ter past meadows of buttercups and cows. After about 5 minutes the whole hillside bursts into a sunball of broom, and the road twists to the right beside a clearing where it is easy to park and slip down to the river to picnic and cool warm feet. The road now begins to climb, past more cows, more meadows, until, after 15 mins, it reaches **Vallter**, a single building with a bar and restaurant not always open. Park and walk behind it over the hills among the last trees, the edelweiss, the golden pasqueflowers and the deep blue gentians.

Pasqueflowers in Vallter

OLOT

15. Catalan Arts and Crafts

Paintings of the Olot School, 'Modernista' and Romanesque architecture, art and craft galleries.

Olot, capital of the Garrotxa region, 35 miles (56.3km) north-west of Girona, is set among spent volcanoes beneath the Pyrenees. Cool, moist and green, the country atmosphere of the region can be appreciated along the banks of the River Fluvia which runs through the south of the town. In the last century this landscape nourished a recognisable school of painting, which was romantic and rural.

This day in Olot traces the artists and their legacy and provides an excuse to get to know a typical Catalan town too often passed by. Monday is a good day to visit, as it is market day, and as a result the **museum** closes not on Monday, but on Tuesday (craft markets are also held intermittently throughout the summer). On arrival in the town, either via Santa Coloma or Besalú, keep going until you reach the tourist information centre next to the three-storey neo-classical Hospice. Turn down Carrer Marià Vayreda opposite, and park; there is always space.

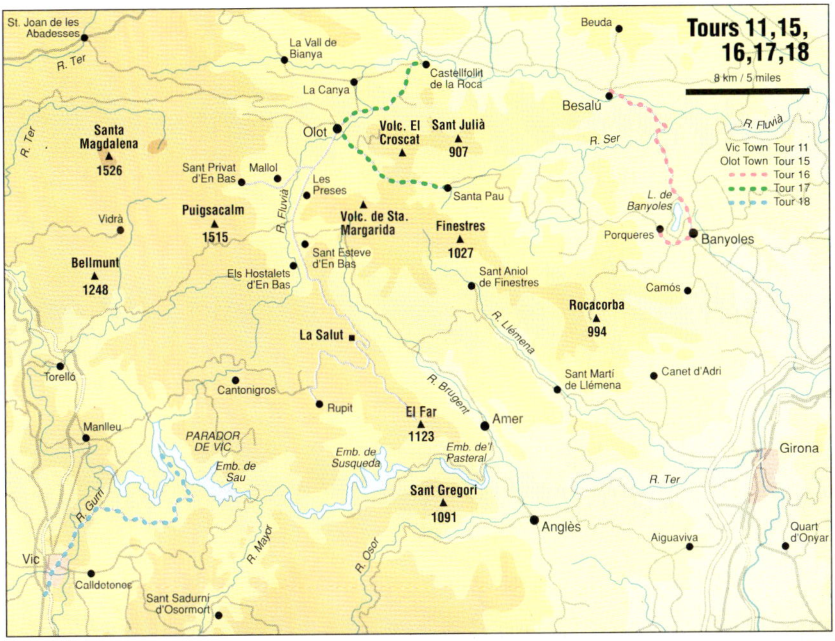

The parallel street is **Carrer Joaquim Vayreda**: he and his brother Marià were central to the Olot School. Their family home is in this street, north of the post office, opposite which is **El Arte Cristiano**, a factory making statues of saints which Joaquim (1843–94) established with the other major figure of the school, Josep Berga i Boix (1837–1914). Marià became better known as a writer: the town library in nearby Carrer Anselm Clave bears his name. Return to the **Hospice** where the *comarcal* museum is housed on the third floor, reached via the central courtyard by stairs or lift. This is an excellent museum, showing the social and political history of the area, its crafts (clog making, saint making) and industries. It also explains how the town's art school was started in the 18th century to provide design ideas for the new textile mills. The Olot school of painters came together a century later and there are fine examples of their work, as well as sculptures, particularly those of Miquel Blay (1866–1936).

The main street in the town is named after Blay. It is up past the church of **St Esteve**, an unattractive building with over-gilded side chapels and an El Greco hidden somewhere in its bowels. Blay's lasting contribution to the street is **Casa Solà-Morales**, designed by the *Modernista* architect Domènech i Montaner, for which he provided the beautifully demure maidens to support the balcony. Unfortunately the interior is not open to the public, however some interiors inspired by the Olot School may soon be seen at a new museum which is being prepared in Casa Trinxeria, 29, Carrer de Sant Esteve.

The shopping streets are in the opposite direction, behind St Esteve. To the right of the church runs **Carrer Carmen**, the main commercial street, with pavements too narrow to contain pedestrians. Across it runs Baix de Tura, leading to **Our Lady of Tura**, the town's favourite church whose statue was recently revealed to be Romanesque. The street ends at Plaça Major, beyond which is the Carmen Convent and the original Fine Arts School, still functioning.

Parallel to Carmen, and running up to the left of St Esteve, is **Carrer Sastre**, Tailor Street, and though some tailors remain, this is now mainly given over to art and craft galleries and shops. Much of today's art in Olot is mediocre, but dealers and painters still come here. A work from a top local artist – Garralda or Colldecarrera – may fetch high prices. The Vayredas, incidentally, are still at it. Marian and Josep Maria, who are cousins, both paint.

For a meal, and a final insight into the world of the Olot School, take the c152 Santa Coloma de Farners road out of town and turn left after about half a mile (800m) where **Font Moixina** is signposted. Drive down this lane to the **Deu Restaurant**, which has stuffed potato specialities and walls lined with modern paintings.

Before or after your meal, continue on past Font Moixina to the old farms near the much-painted little chapel of **La Salut**. On the edge of a damp, dappled wood, old women still fetch water in pitchers, geese at their feet: it looks much the same as when it was painted by Joaquim Vayreda and Josep Berga i Boix.

16. Picnic at Banyoles; Dinner in Besalú

Banyoles town and its lake, the Romanesque church of Santa Maria at Porqueres, prehistoric bones in the archaeological museum and the medieval town of Besalú.

A day by a lake has quite a different feel to a day by the sea. For a picnic take a small French loaf *(de quart de kilo)* for two people. Slice it lengthways, rub garlic, oil and tomatoes into one side, stick it back together and wrap it up in a bag. Buy some sausage *(xoriço, botifarra, mortadella, fuet)*, goat's or dry Manchego cheese, some olives and whatever fruit is in season. Include a bottle of wine, pink if it can be kept cool, or *gasosa* (lemonade).

Banyoles is about 15 miles (24km) east of Olot and 12 miles (19.3km) north of Girona on the C150. Its warm, blue lake on the edge of the volcanic zone is 5 miles (8km) round. Skirt the lake to the left and head for the bank opposite Banyoles town and yacht club. Just beyond **Porqueres** are wide grassy banks overhung with willows: the perfect spot to get out the Frisbee and set down the gingham table-cloth. The water is deep, turquoise, slightly sulphurous and a little warm. It is, in fact, fed not by rivers but by underground springs. It is quite safe for bathing.

The warm, blue lake at Banyoles

Before leaving the lake, take a trip around it on one of the goose-prowed boats (400 pesetas) which sail from beside the wire-mesh pens where giant carp are kept and fed a diet of unshelled peanuts. When restlessness sets in, walk along to the beautiful 13th-century Romanesque church of **Santa Maria at Porqueres**.

In **Banyoles** itself, just off the colonnaded main square are two museums. The **Darder Museum** is the bequest of a former mayor, a polymath who collected and stuffed animals from all over the world, and added several mummies, including that of an African warrior which caused an upset during the Olympic Games. In the **archaeological museum** in the Pia Almoina (almshouse) there is evidence of the prehistoric animals which once roamed the area, but its greatest treasure is a small jawbone showing that man lived here 100,000 years ago.

In the early evening drive 10 miles (16km) north on the C150 to **Besalú**, a former county town and the best-preserved medieval enclave in the region. Follow the signs to the centre of town and park in the large dusty square before the church of Sant Pere.

This is an easy town to walk around: the rewards come thick and fast. The helpful information office is in Plaça de la Llibertat, the colonnaded main square. Ask for the key to the *mikwah* (Jewish ritual baths). This is not much more than an empty stone room, but it has a rarity value: only three exist in Europe. The information office will also give the next visiting time for the impressive church of **Sant Pere**, all that is left of the town's monastery after the 19th-century dissolutions. Casa dels Cornellà, in the oposite corner of the square, is an unusual Romanesque secular building. The church of Sant Vicenç is also worth a visit. Antique shops in the Plaça Sant Pere and by the main road should be perused.

Have a drink on the terrace at the back of the **Cúria Real**, in the corner of the Plaça Major, but for dinner go to the **Pont Vell**. This restaurant is just by the town's distinctive fortified bridge which

The medieval enclave of Besalú

17. Volcanic Walks

A gentle day of walking along well-signposted footpaths with lunch or dinner in Santa Pau.

The volcanic zone centred in the Garrotxa is a distinctive region of dark green cones, forested hills, that rise and fall all around the town of Olot and east towards Castellfollit, an extraordinary village which perches on a basalt outcrop above the Fluvia River. The eruptions are not officially declared over, but there has been nothing major for 11,000 years. The phenomenon has also affected the architecture, for the basalt rock gives the region's sturdy *masies*, the farmhouses, their dark, blotchy faces.

To start a day – or even just a few hours – of exploration, begin at the Casa del Volcans signposted just off the C152 road leading out of Olot towards **Santa Coloma de Farners**. This information centre provides a good leaflet in English, with map. From here turn back into town and take the **Santa Pau** road (GE524) signposted on the through road. Within the next 6 miles (9.6km) there is a choice of walks through the woods and round the volcanic humps, all of which are signposted in the traditional local way: parallel red-and-white stripes painted on trees or rocks. When painted as a cross they indicate where not to go. As several trails intersect here, each has a different colour instead of red. First stop along this road is **Fageda d'en Jordà**, a fairy-glen beechwood. A poem dedicated to it by the 19th-century poet Joan Maragall can be found at the entrance, opposite a car park.

Santa Pau

Two miles (3.2km) further on, past the Can Xell Restaurant, is the Margarida bar, and just round the corner on the right is parking space for the crater of **Santa Margarida**. This is a good volcano to visit as it is possible to climb up its rim and look down its grassy slopes to the little church in its centre. To find out what the inside of these volcanic lumps is like, drive down the tinder track behind the Margarida bar. This leads to the **Croscat volcano**. Its great dark centre has been scoured out, leaving a bleak moonscape over which lorries lumber back and forth.

Finally, continue driving for a few minutes more down this road to **Santa Pau**. This is a charming medieval enclave built around an arcaded square. Park outside the town hall and walk over the bridge into the old village. On the way, visit the general store (*Alimentacion*), which has hardly changed in 100 years. If you are hungry, enter the **Cal Sastre**, the small restaurant towards the end of the arcade. The set menu is cheap and comes with large helpings of fresh vegetables, of which this region is proud.

18. Valley of Flowers

A leisurely, rural route centred on the Val d'en Bas between the town of Olot and the hills to the south where the Fluvia starts to flow. The sanctuaries in their heights provide spectacular views and good lunching spots, popular with Catalans on Sunday.

From Olot, take the c152 Santa Coloma de Farners road out of town. Follow the sign from the main road to **Sant Privat d'en Bas** 4 miles (6.4km) west. This pretty little place consists entirely of its cobbled main square, and sometimes the only person visible is a painter at an easel. On the way back to the main road, turn up to **Mallol**, a collection of creaking timbered farm buildings, where there is a grand view of the pancake-flat valley stretching out between dark green volcanic cones to the left and the high, flat-topped escarpment of Puigcalm to the right.

Back on the main road, continue south, taking the right fork (c153) signposted to Barcelona and Vic. A few minutes afterwards is **Els Hostalets d'en Bas**, set back from the road on the right, the most flower-filled village in this part of Spain. The 18th-century wood lintels above the doors bear the names of the original inhabitants. Continuing past Hostalets, the road begins to wind upwards.

Els Hostalets d'en Bas

Els Hostalets d'en Bas

After about 20mins there is a sign to the sanctuary of **Mare de Deu de la Salut**, a pleasant spot with dramatic views. Continue for a few more minutes to the café at Coll de Condreu (3,275ft/1,000m) and turn left to **Mare de Deu del Far**. A fine 15-minute hillside drive beside sloping meadows and among cool woods ends at a simple church whose interior offers no more comfort than that afforded by a stone cave. Park here and walk through to the sanctuary (open all year) where there are spectacular views down over the valley left behind. To the south lies the Susqueda dam which which was constructed to stem the annual floods in Girona.

Lunch in the sanctuary restaurant is served in large brown bowls and might include *ànec amb bolets* (duck with mushrooms), *llenguado i llagostins* (sole with prawns) or *senglar sofregit* (stewed boar), all reasonably priced. Or, for a light lunch, try just cold meats and salad (*amanida i embotits*).

Our last stop for the day is **Rupit**, 10 miles (16km) away on the road to Vic. This is a village with a real mountain feel, popular with owners of second homes. Park by the bar and bakery (*Forn de pa*) on arrival in the village and walk up around the back of the buildings perched under extraordinary rock formations. In the village look out for little shops like the one opposite the church, selling home-cured hams and *Ratafia*, a spirit flavoured with herbs. On the way back, cross the Indiana Jones-style footbridge swaying breezily above the River Rupit. Have a coffee in the bakery by the car park where the ovens produce great crispy *coques*. Return either via the Val d'en Bas, or by continuing to the city of Vic, a pleasant, 45-minute mountain drive away.

View from Mare de Deu del Far

Shopping

In summer, at the height of the tourist season, the visitors who throng the resorts are catered for by boutiques, delicatessens, gift shops and supermarkets, but Catalonia is a nation of small businessmen and shopkeepers who provide the backbone of the daily economy.

The small town or village shop offers the greatest rewards, both for souvenir hunting and for an insight into the lives of the local people. Prices are not necessarily more expensive than in supermarkets, and are sometimes cheaper: price controls are not fully enforced. Shopkeepers will spend time with their customers, which can madden people in a hurry, and will gift wrap even the most trifling purchase. Village general stores (*comistibles*) can be fascinating Aladdin's caves, selling biscuits, birthday candles, baskets of vegetables from the local allotments (*hortes*), fresh eggs, espadrilles, porous pitchers to keep water cool, litres of cologne, Barcelona football club stickers, envelopes, pulses, postcards and pots.

Blanes market

Markets

Weekly markets (see 'Hours and Holidays' in the *What to Know* section for dates and places) are still an important part of both the local economies and the rhythm of life. They provide the necessities in fresh food, and in linen and clothes, as well as hardware.

Some markets, such as **Sant Feliu's**, have a good name for clothes, but in general the quality of market clothes is poor and the prices are high (there is no bartering). Hardware stalls are worth a browse, for cheap chopping boards, wooden spoons and spatulas, pestles and mortars, or such items as sugar-burning irons which are not easy to find at home. There may also be a stall selling bowls and other implements made of olive wood.

Herbalists' stalls will sell herbs for infusions and jars of pollen to sprinkle on salads. There are also liable to be local jewellery and gift items such as small bottles of coloured sand or pocket sundials: every year brings new novelties. Look out, too, for special markets, such as the craft markets in Palafrugell and Olot.

Ceramics and Antiques

Ceramics are the best value souvenirs. Earthenware cooking pots and kitchen bowls are extremely cheap and hardware shops in any town or village sell them. There are also roadside emporiums thoughout the province, which are impossible to miss. Any space in the car should be filled with great garden pots and ornaments (it is worth noting that the pots are rarely frost-resistant and often fall apart come spring). Most ceramic shops sell alabaster ornaments as well.

La Bisbal, 17 miles (27km) east of Girona, is the principal ceramic centre: some three dozen shops line its main streets, and in some it is possible to watch potters at work, and kilns firing. Most of the pottery is decorated, and it ranges from the traditional tiles showing industries and crafts, and plates with fish and wind roses, to modern vases, sculptures and lamp stands. **Quart**, 5 miles (8km) south-east of Girona has a long tradition of black- and green-glazed pottery, and again it may be possible to see one of the giant old gas-fired kilns roaring into life.

Ceramics make some of the most interesting antique buys. Plain pots look truly rustic, plates and tiles are pretty, apothecary jars are attractive. There are antique shops on the Girona side of the road through **La Bisbal**, which have some enormous examples. Antiques sold in market stalls – keys, lamps, copper pans, fire irons, farm implements – tend to be on the expensive side. **Cadaqués** and **Sant Feliu** have large antique shops and, further inland, visit the shops in **Peralada**, **Besalú** and **Ripoll**.

Leather and Clothes

Leather goods can be an excellent buy, whether in the form of clothes, shoes, belts, bags or watch straps. **La Platja d'Aro** has the major retail outlets and weekend shoppers come from Barcelona. But leather goods are in evidence in all markets and towns. In **Girona** the main clothes shops are in the new town around Carrer Santa Clara. Shoes have been getting dearer, but there are still some good buys, both for style and for quality, especially in soft leather.

Food and Drink

Olives and nuts should be snapped up. Virgin olive oil is also worth bringing home, as is a good bottle of wine vinegar. Strings of garlic are at their best early in the year. Jars of salted anchovies are a speciality of **L'Escala**. They should be boned and washed thoroughly, soaked in olive oil for 24 hours, taken out and served with a sprinkling of vinegar. (Soak the bones in milk for 20mins, then dust with flour and fry, to make a Bombay duck-like appetiser.)

Local biscuits are made in many places, often with almonds, pine nuts, or honey. The Trias company in **Santa Coloma** make the most exciting, but **Arbúcies**, **Camprodon**, **La Bisbal** and other towns all have specialities. The sweet-toothed will like *turron*, a honey and nougat speciality. Scotch is the only spirit not worth buying, and no alcohol is worth buying in duty-free shops, as it can all be bought so much more cheaply locally. Brandy is certainly a sound investment: Osborne or Carlos III are perfectly acceptable cognacs. A local spirit is *Ratafia*, which is anise flavoured with herbs. Other specialities, such as Liqueur de Núria, should be avoided. *Cava* and still wines are good buys.

Market antiques in Blanes

Dining

For the ordinary Catalan, Sundays and holidays are occasions for family get-togethers when lunch is a protracted meal, especially if it can be enjoyed outdoors, barbecued, either in the garden, on the beach or in the countryside.

Food for free is always appreciated and it adds to the outdoor feeling: asparagus plucked from the wayside in spring; mussels boiled on the rocks in pans of seawater in summer; mushrooms from the forest floor in autumn; snails in the fields after a rain shower all the year round. Add to this fish caught on the line, or partridge and quail bagged in the hills and the result is the ingredients of Catalonia's particular regional style: *mar i muntanya*, food from the mountains and from the sea.

Dishes will combine chicken and prawns, beef and prunes, rabbit and snails, trout and ham, aubergines stuffed with anchovies. A platter of cold meats (*embotits*) may be followed by a *graellada* of fried fish; a dish of shredded salt cod (*esqueixada*) may precede a stew of wild boar (*senglar*). Pasta, eggs and rice are all commonly used. After a while it is hard to think of cannelloni (*canalons*) as anything but a Catalan dish, especially when stuffed with seafood. Eggs are sometimes stirred into soups and stews, or made into an omelette (*truita*) filled with potatoes, spinach or cod. Black rice (*arrós negre*) gets its charcoal blue-black colour from the squid ink in which it is cooked.

Meat and Fish

Meat in general is expensive, but the cuts are good and the butchers expect to prepare it any way the customer wants. Pork products are a staple and pork fat is a basis for many dishes. Pigs' trotters (*peus*

de porc) are a delicacy, but many may find them unpleasantly fatty. Lamb (*xai*) and veal (*vedella*) are good but expensive. Rabbit (*conill*) is common: in restaurants it is grilled and served with *allioli*, garlic mayonnaise. Chicken (*pollastre*), which can have a wonderful flavour, is sold both in butchers and with charcuterie in delicatessens. There are many varieties of sausage (*salsitxa*), some to be sliced and eaten raw (*botifarra* pork sausage or salami-like *fuet*), others for cooking (*xoriço*).

A classic stew is *escudella i carn d'olla*, made with a variety of meats and vegetables. In farms and country houses in days gone by it was cooked over the fire in a pot and kept going seven days a week. It should be served in two parts, the juices as a soup to start, followed by the meaty stew.

Seafood is not as abundant on the coast as one might expect. The daily market in Girona is generally much cheaper and has more variety than on the coast. Even such traditional food as salt cod (*bacallà*) is often imported. Sold in stiff strips, it needs soaking for 24 hours with a change of water halfway through. Sardines and mackerel are cheap but fresh anchovies are not easy to find fresh outside the main towns. Hake (*lluç*) is the most commonly served fish. Turbot, bass and mullett are all dear. Mussels are cheap, lobster and squid are expensive, crabs are small. The principal fish dishes are *graellada*, a mixed grill, and *sarsuela*, a stew. A *suquet* is a soup made of white fish only. In Tossa *cim-i-tomba* is a fish speciality. *El niu* is a delicacy of Palafrugell, based on cod's stomach, and stacked with game, meat, fish and vegetables.

Market Produce

There are many self-catering villas and apartments on the coast and cooking in the home gives a great opportunity to try fresh produce, particularly vegetables which can be woefully absent from restaurant menus. Firm, green tomatoes and sweet red peppers form the basis of much local cuisine. They are the essence of *samfaina*, a *ratatouille*-like sauce made with aubergines and courgettes which goes well with chicken.

Olives are definitely worth buying and a stall may have up to two dozen varieties: sweet, bitter, black, green, pitted, spiced, in a garlic marinade. Taste before buying and try 100gm each of three or four varieties. Broad beans, *faves*, are cooked *a la catalana* with black pudding, sausage and bacon. When they are fresh, *faves* are wonderful in salads with mint. Broad beans are ready in spring, and are just one thing to look out for in the markets as the seasons change.

Fruit may be served in place of a dessert (usually a *crema catalana*, a local *crême brulée*, which if made on the premises in individual earthenware bowls is unbeatable). Strawberries can be bought by the kilo for half of the year and should be eaten with *cava* sparkling wine. Nuts are also served for dessert, mixed with dried fruit, and market stalls have a good selection of hazel nuts, cashews, almonds, pistachios, peanuts and pine nuts, as well as less common varieties such as ground almonds, used for making the local milk drink, *orxata*.

Snacks

Tapes (*tapas* in Castilian), small plates of free food to accompany a drink, are not a Catalan tradition. Many bars do, however, have bowls of different appetisers which are served in small platefuls (*racions*), and a light meal can be easily made up of several portions of different dishes. These might include small fish in oil (*boquerones*), tiny squid cooked in their own ink (*popets*), wild mushrooms (*bolets*), spinach tortilla (*truita de espinache*). Any of these with a plate of *pa amb tomàquet*, slabs of country bread rubbed with oil and tomato, can make a whole meal.

A light lunchtime snack in a restaurant could simply be a salad (*amanida*). A Catalan salad, eaten as a first course, is a plate of lettuce, tomato, onion and olives with a variety of cold meats. These meats, often cured locally, might include several kinds of ham, sausage and salami. With *pa amb tomàquet*, such a salad can be a meal in itself.

Restaurants

Lunch is eaten between two and three in the afternoon. In summer people tend to eat dinner late, not contemplating a meal until around 10pm. In out-of-the-way country places, however, people will probably eat by about 9pm.

Catalans take great pride in where they eat. The best places are not necessarily the most ethnic looking or the most expensive. As a general rule, the further from the coast the better the food, but if you want to find good coastal restaurants, look for those with Barcelona and Girona registered cars in the car parks, often out of town alongside main roads. If a restaurant is popular with the locals it will be good and usually inexpensive, too. Though they may lack an intimate ambience, some of the better hotels, which can employ a cook all year round, have good restaurants.

From 1961 until his death in 1979 Josep Mercader, from Cadaqués, ran the Motel (now Hotel) **Ampurdan**, still functioning just outside Figueres. He is largely credited for giving Catalan cuisine its modern prestige by combining traditional local elements, particularly from his own Empordà region, with innovative new touches. Innovation has also been the hallmark of the **Eldorado Petit** in Sant Feliu de Guíxols, which is the original of the top Barcelona restaurant of the same name, and in La Platja d'Aro Carlo Camós has made a reputation for himself and his style of cooking at the **Big Rock**.

Wine

Catalans enjoy wine with meals and they drink it regularly rather than heavily: a visiting *bon viveur* from a highly taxed northern country may be upset to see half-drunk bottles left on restaurant tables. At its cheapest, wine comes out of the barrel in local stores or in *bodegues* and customers take their own bottles to be filled. The three colours, red, pink and white are called *negre*, *rosat* and *blanc*. Sweet dessert wines also come from the barrel. They are *moscatell*, *ranci* and *garnatxa*, brews which range from syrupy to delicious. Most wines are red and they can be heavy and high in alcohol. None of the barrel wines travels well: it is better to buy *denominación de origen* wines to bring home.

Table wine from the Empordà-Costa Brava *denominación de origen* is served in many restaurants, and is easily found in the shops. Oliveda is the main brand. It is cheap and drinkable. Ricardell, at Pont de Molins, also makes a respectable table wine. A good *vi novell*, a kind of Beaujolais Nouveau is produced every year and is still in the shops at Easter. Reds are often drunk chilled, but those who find them a bit heavy should try the pink: the whites lack crispness, though Peralada's slightly pricey Pescador Blanc is popular. *Cava*, Catalonia's Champagne-method wines, are so cheap they can be drunk like ordinary wine: at cafés in Peralada, customers drink nothing else. Individual-sized bottles, *benjamins*, are an idea for an aperitif.

Nightlife

Night-time entertainments start late. Anything from a circus to a classical concert is not likely to begin before 11pm, sometimes midnight. Discos, too, don't really get going until the next day has begun. Nightlife is a preserve of the coast, and is not to be found inland except during festivals. The two major night spots are **Lloret de Mar** and **La Platja d'Aro** (see Tour 8 *A Night Out in La Platja d'Aro*) which boasts the greatest concentration of discos on the coast. The towns' summer crowds choose these towns just as much for the discos as for the sun and the sea. But young people from all over the province, and from Barcelona, make up the basic clientele, keeping a few venues open after the tourists have gone. In the summer months, discos spring up in all the resorts, but only in the more established resorts do they stay open in winter, and then only on weekends.

Lloret's nightlife is centred around Carrer La Riera, where bars, pubs and night spots can make any nationality feel at home (English language films are shown on the patio of the Queen Vic). Neon and lasers light the skies and laser shows are laid on at the

Revolution and **Tropics**, the town's best known night spot which is open all year round. In these busy resorts, discos try to select their clientele by giving away tickets in the streets to the kind of people they want inside. Without a ticket you must pay to get in. Entrance fees vary between 1,000 and 2,000 pesetas. Drinks are around four times the usual price. Discos close about 5am.

Live Music and Gambling

Live music is also on offer in the larger resorts. There is jazz and Latin American music (big band leader Xavier Cugat came from Girona). In folk music Lluís Llach is the most important local figure. In Palafrugell's resorts of **Calella** and **Llafranc** *havaneres* sea shanties are occasions of jollity which the audience can, apparently, only appreciate while drinking *cremat*, coffee with rum. Flamenco has nothing to do with Catalonia, but shows are put on from Llança to Blanes. Old-fashioned funfairs and big tops are installed in the larger resorts.

Lloret de Mar has an enormous cabaret venue for song-and-dance evenings in the Gran Palace. The casino in the Hotel Casino complex offers *boule*, roulette, blackjack, *chemin de fer* and one-armed bandits. Gamblers need passports here and at the casino in the castle at Peralada. Gambling, banned by Franco, is a relatively new experience in Spain. (Catalonia's third casino is at Sant Pere de Ribes.) Casinos are open from about 7pm–4am.

Luciano Pavarotti, among the summer stars

Music Festivals

Every summer music festivals are held in some 20 venues, and they attract a wide range of top performers, from Liza Minelli to Luciano Pavarotti. The charm of these concerts, which are well advertised, is partly in the venues themselves: serene monasteries such as Ripoll and Vilabertran, solid churches such as Torroella de Montgrí and Palamós, castles such as Castell d'Aro and Peralada.

The Catalan opera singers José Carreras and Montserrat Caballé usually perform at one of the events. Julio Iglesias has appeared, as has the National Ballet of Spain. Some of the smaller venues are well suited to chamber orchestra recitals: I Musici has played at Vilabertran and Christopher Hogwood's Academy of Ancient Music has performed Bach at Sant Feliu de Guixols.

Special Events

Every town and village in the province has a main feast day, *a festa major*, and even small communities can produce a lively occasion. A *sardana* band is central to the proceedings, and a number of towns will bring out their giants and 'bigheads' to dance for the crowds. Mediocre rock bands may be organised through a local impressario, and they will take over when the *sardana* has stopped – or the *sardana* band may turn into a Latin American combo when the sun goes down. Nobody is expected to go to bed. Small children fall asleep in their parents' arms. The next day even dogs wake late.

The *sardana* is a special **Catalan dance**: formal, popular and a continuing source of national pride. Dances are held in every town and village at some point in the year. Everyone takes part, holding hands, forming circles and, with a concentration that makes them look far too serious, counting the beats to which they skip and jump. The origins of the dance may go back to the ancient Greeks, but in its present shape it dates from the 19th century. It was then that **Pep Ventura** re-organised the band, or *cobla*, defined the structure of the music and wrote hundreds of tunes which were either original works or adaptations of popular songs, such as *El*

'Sardana' at La Bisbal

cant dels ocells (some *sardanes* are sung).

The *sardana* band, or *cobla*, is made up of 11 players: one double-bass player and five brass players who stand behind five seated woodwind players, one of whom (the leader) plays a pipe and taps out the rhythm on a small drum strapped to his elbow. It is the *tenora*, the woodwind instrument, that is responsible for the haunting *sardana* sound.

Catalans are taught the dance at school, so everyone knows what to do. Lining up, men and women alternately, they hold hands and form ever growing circles. The dance is complicated, and it involves accurate counting of the steps, which accounts for the serious look on the participants' faces. If everyone ends the dance on the right foot and the right note, it is a success. There are a set number of pieces a *cobla* might play. If there is more than one band, or the event goes on for a long time – they can last up to three days – the meeting is called an *aplec* (a reunion). *Aplecs* can be large gatherings, like the one held in **Olot each July** which is attended by bands from France and dancing goes on all day.

Giants and Hobby Horses

For most of the year, **town giants**, originally mascots of the local trades guilds, reside in the town halls. Reaching some 12ft (4m) tall, they tend to come as a pair: a king and a queen, a shepherd and a shepherdess, a sun and a moon. At festival time, strong men get beneath their skirts and lift up their wood frame bases for the dance, whooping and dipping and swirling through the streets and across the squares, attended by 'bigheads' (*capgrossos*) and accompanied by a small band playing ancient, rustic instruments called *gralles*, and a small drum, the *tabal*.

They come out at Santa Creu in **Figueres** in April, on Sant Narcis, **Girona**'s two-week-long October *festa major*, and in September in **Olot**'s Festa del Tura, one of the largest giants' parades which includes *nans* (dwarfs) and *cavallins* (hobbyhorses). In fact the whole Garrotxa region around Olot has a quite distinct folkloric flavour with special characters and dances. The hobbyhorses put in their most colourful appearance on Whit Sunday at **Sant Feliu de Pallerols**, just to the south of Olot, when they are joined by a kind of devil-mule called the *mulassa*. The following day, Whit Monday, in **Riudaura**, a village just west of Olot, the *Ball de Gambeto* is danced by men dressed in frock coats and top hats and women in white caps and shawls.

The fiesta Semana Santa in Verges

Christmas Crèches and Easter Rituals

The main treat for children at Christmas is not the day itself, but **Epiphany**, 6 January, the day of the Three Wise Men, or the Three Kings (*Els Tres Reis*). Traditionally, they arrive on horseback, or sometimes by boat, and distribute presents. Christmas proper is simply a family feast day which centres around an elaborately stuffed turkey, a bird which is never otherwise seen on the table. Living crèches, or *tableaux vivants,* are acted out by villagers at Christmastime. Castell d'Aro, Bàscara (just north of Girona) and Capmany all stage these scenes of the holy nativity.

The next major event on the winter calendar is the pre-Lenten **carnival**. Most towns and villages have fancy dress dances, but a major *charivari* disrupts Roses, Lloret de Mar and La Platja d'Aro. One of the province's most ancient and intriguing events is the **Dance of Death** enacted on Maundy Thursday in Verges, 22 miles (35.4km) north-east of Girona. Thought to echo a 14th-century plague rite, it features men and boys dressed as skeletons (white bones painted on black costumes) who dance through the streets stopping every now and then to point to a clock's minute hand approaching midnight. This torchlit procession completes the evening rituals which begin, at around 10.30pm, with the procession of a statue of Christ crucified accompanied by a legion of local Roman soldiers. A **Passion Play** takes place in the square.

The Roman soldiers, called *manaies* and kitted out by various societies and districts of the towns, have been swelling. They turn out at Camprodon, and nearly 1,000 of them form the most dramatic part of Girona's Good Friday parade, taking the crucified Christ from the church of Sant Feliu to the cathedral. There is also a Passion Play at **Sant Hilari Sacalm**, involving a dramatic crucifixion.

Saint George

William Shakespeare was born and died on 23 April, the day of **St George**, patron saint of England and Catalonia. It is also the day that Don Quixote's author, Miguel Cervantes, died. In honour of the saint and the writer, **Sant Jordi** is celebrated in Catalonia as a day of books and red roses, the flower of the saint.

Most towns set up stalls in their *rambles*, selling books about Catalonia, while others sell single roses wrapped in silver paper. In the Rambla in Girona, shops move their goods out on to tressle tables on the streets, a figure of fun is balanced overhead on a pole which straddles two facing balconies and in the evening literary prizes are presented for the year's works in Catalan.

Midsummer Pageants

Since Franco's death, the midsummer's eve fires of Sant Joan have burned hotly in Catalonia. Most dramatically, on 23 June, St John's Eve, fires are lit on the summit of **Mount Canigó**, just over the border in France. From there flaming torches are taken by runners, even cars, to the towns in the plains and valleys around about. As darkness falls on the longest day, the valleys begin to twinkle with bonfire light. Around them there are *coques* of Sant Joan, great trenchers of cake, to be eaten with *cava* sparkling wine. On the coast, an important saint is **La Mare de Déu del Carme**, whose day falls in mid-July. Her effigy is carried in procession and then out to sea for a blessing by fishermen as well as naval ratings, for she is patron saint of all sailors. She is celebrated in Llançà, Cadaqués, Roses, Llafranc, Palamós and Sant Feliu de Guíxols. Lloret has its own sea-borne pageant of local saint, **Santa Cristina**, on 24 July. In the morning a flotilla collects her from the beach beneath her hillside church and transports her to the resort where she spends a day of feasting and celebration. At day's end the flotilla takes her back home.

National Day

Catalonia's national day, **La Diada**, on September 11 is also its most political day. It celebrates the fall of Barcelona in 1714 to the incoming Bourbon monarch, Felipe V, and the subsequent loss of rights and privileges. It is a day of giants, fireworks, *sardanes*, political protests and much singing of Els Segadors (the national Catalan anthem) to swell hearts with nostalgia and pride.

What to Know

Practical Information

GETTING THERE

By Air

The Costa Brava is about 1½ hours from the UK by air. Girona-Costa Brava airport, a small airport with few facilities 11 miles (17.7km) south of the city, only handles charter flights. Prices from the UK are relatively cheap and depend on the season, time of day and airport of origin. The cheapest flights are at the most anti-social hours. There is no public transport from the airport, though package tours are met by coaches. The taxi ride to the centre of Girona takes about 20 minutes.

Iberia, the national airline, is the principal operator in Barcelona and it offers money-saving deals which can be as good as the charter fares. (London office, 071-437 5622; Girona office, (972) 20 58 00.) It also offers fly-drive deals.

The train from Barcelona's El Prat airport, via Sants and Gràcia stations, takes about 1½ hours to Girona. The line is coded R1, and it continues up to Figueres, not meeting the coast until Llançà near the French border.

Alternatively, for travellers to the south of the coast, the Vapor de la Costa goes from Barcelona along the Maresme coast turning inland just before Blanes and meeting up with the R1 just before Girona, at Maçanet.

By Rail

All trains from Paris to Barcelona and Madrid stop at Girona. From Paris Austerlitz to Girona is about 10 hours. The trains cross the border at Portbou where you have to change, except when travelling in a luxury Talgo which has adaptable wheels. Spain laid down a different guage to keep the French out: new high speed links are planned to bring them in.

By Road

By motorway, the border is about 13 hours from the English Channel ports, either via Lyons or Bordeaux. The journey can be made in a day but it is better to allow for an overnight stop.

The winding coastal road (the N114 in France becoming the C252 in Spain) crosses the border at Portbou and is pretty but slow. The main routes into Spain at the north of the Costa Brava are the parallel national route N11 and the A7 motorway, coming from Perpignan over the border at La Jonquera. Both are busy in summer and though the motorway queues can be longer, they move faster. Motorways in Spain are subject to toll charges. The 40-mile (64.3-km) stretch between the border and Girona costs a few hundred pesetas.

Bus services run from most large European cities. Eurolines have a regular service from London's Victoria coach station, which reaches Girona in about 25 hours (Tel: 071-730 0202). They have links with the local Spanish company, Julià.

Visas and Passports

A national identity card is sufficient for visitors from EC countries, Switzerland and Malta; passports for everyone else. No vaccinations are required unless coming from a country where cholera, smallpox or yellow fever have not been eliminated.

EC citizens may stay up to three months but after that need a temporary resident's permit, for which they apply at their local police station.

Customs

You are allowed to bring into Catalonia any amount of money, plus items for personal use – a radio, musical instrument, bicycle. Two cameras are allowed but only five rolls of film, which is expensive in Spain. If the customs think you will sell anything in your possession, you may have to sign a declaration that you won't, and leave a deposit which you can collect on leaving.

You are only allowed to take 20,000 pesetas out of the country. In general, the customs seem fairly relaxed (sometimes there is nobody at all at the customs post on the coast road) and passports are not usually stamped.

TRAVEL ESSENTIALS

What to Wear

In summer, as for any warm climate, take cool, comfortable clothes and nothing thicker than a sweatshirt or cardigan. In spring or autumn, evenings can be quite cool and a thick jersey or jacket will be needed, plus waterproof shoes and umbrella: it doesn't rain often but when it does it can be torrential. Take sensible shoes if you intend to walk. Dress is informal, but beachwear stands out in towns and cities. Beach styles range from baggy shorts and one-piece costumes to nothing at all, depending on where you are and what you feel like.

Weather

The sun is seldom unpleasantly hot in summer, but the cool heights of the nearby Pyrenees mean the weather is not always settled. If grey clouds descend they may last two or three days. A north wind, the *Tramontana*, can strike at any time and may last two or three days. But much of the weather is local, and if it is gloomy or rainy in one resort, it may be sunny in another only a dozen or so miles away.

Money Matters

Spanish currency is the peseta (pesseta in Catalan). Coins are in denominations of 1 peseta to 500 pesetas, and notes from 500 to 10,000 pesetas. There are just under 200 pesetas to the pound. Banks are open in the morning until 2pm but in summer there is no shortage of change (*canvi*) places in resorts, where the bank rate prevails. Travellers' cheques and Eurocheques are safe and need passports for cashing. Cashpoints accept some charge cards with PIN numbers: ask your bank before you go.

Tipping

If in doubt, tip, but don't overdo it. Tipping seems more of a custom than a necessity: 10 pesetas for a coffee, 5–10 per cent for meals or taxis. Also, tip 1–200 pesetas to non-officials who show you around a church or monument: they are usually volunteers.

Weights and Electricity

The metric system is used for all weights and measurements. Electricity is 220 volts, except in a few villages which have not yet been converted from 110. Small, two-round-pin plugs are standard so adapters are needed for hair dryers etc. Power and light are sometimes on different circuits.

Time Differences

For most of the year Spanish time is one hour ahead of UK time. Clocks are put forward an hour at the end of March, about the same time as Britain, and put back one hour at the end of September, about a month before Britain.

GOVERNMENT & ECONOMY

Spain is a constitutional monarchy under King Juan Carlos. In 1989 the Spanish Socialist Party, PSOE, was re-elected in Madrid for a third term. Catalonia, of which Girona and the Costa Brava are a part, is one of several semi-autonomous regions. It is governed by the Generalitat in Barcelona, which is led by Jordi Pujol of the conservative Convergència i Unió party. The PSOE is the ruling party in both Barcelona and Girona councils.

Girona is one of four Catalonian provinces. The other three are Barcelona, Tarragona and Lleida, all named after the principal cities. Each province is divided into small counties called *comarques*. In Girona these are: La Cerdanya (county town Puigcerdà), El Ripollés (Ripoll), La Garrotxa (Olot), Alt Empordà (Figueres), Baix Empordà (La Bisbal), Pla de L'Estany (Banyoles), El Gironès (Girona), La Selva (Santa Coloma de Farners).

Employment in the region is among the highest in Spain, although much of this is seasonal. The service sector employs 46 per cent of the working population. Tourism has taken people away from the fields and only 10 per cent work on the land, half of which is covered by forest. Girona has Spain's only forestry training school.

The rest of the population work in construction and industry, including food processing, textiles and paper-making – a paper factory belching smoke from a red-and-white stack beside the N-II north of Girona accounts for the pervading unpleasant smell.

HEALTH & EMERGENCIES

Health

Private medical insurance is a good idea. The DHSS E111 forms are supposed to work, but they are both complicated and uncertain.

Chemists are helpful with minor complaints. Called *famàcies*, they display green or red crosses and are usually open from 9am–1pm and 4.30–8pm. They should display notices giving details of a local emergency service; otherwise ask the police. Town halls post surgery hours of clinics. The main towns have hospitals with 24-hour emergency departments.

Apart from sun and alcohol, a change of diet and water may also bring problems. Water is good everywhere: a naturally carbonated bottled water can settle a stomach, though pregnant women are advised not to drink some carbonated mineral waters. Ease gently into the sun: with a slight sea breeze it can seem much weaker than it actually is, and an initial blast of it could ruin a whole holiday.

Police and Crime

The Costa Brava has no great crime problems, but take the usual precautions, especially in tourists areas. Always lock your car, and preferably don't take it into Barcelona (if you must, garage it). Report all thefts. The police emergency number is 091.

HOURS & HOLIDAYS

Business Hours

Most shops and offices open from 9am–1pm and 4pm–8pm from Monday to Friday and shops keep the same hours on Saturday. Banks are generally open from 9am–2pm. In coastal resorts in high season shops often open seven days a week.

Public Holidays

Businesses close for local holidays and town festivals. Banks, shops and museums are closed on the following public holidays:

New Year	1 January
Epiphany	6 January
St Joseph's	19 March
Good Friday	
Easter Monday	
Corpus Christi	
Labour Day	1 May
St James's Day	25 July
Assumption	15 August
National Day	11 September
Columbus Day	12 October
All Saints	1 November
Constitution Day	6 December
Immaculate Conception	8 December
Christmas Day	25 December
St Stephen's Day	26 December

Weekly Markets

Monday: Blanes, Cadaqués, Olot, Torroella de Montgrí.

Tuesday: Besalú, Caldes de Malavella, Castelló d'Empúries, Lloret de Mar, Palamós.

Wednesday: Banyoles, Llançà.

Thursday: Estartit, Figueres, Llagostera, Tossa de Mar, Vic.

Friday: La Bisbal, El Port de la Selva

Saturday: Girona, Vic.

Sunday: L'Escala, Palafrugell, Ribes, Ripoll, Roses, Sant Feliu de Guíxols, Sant Joan de les Abadesses.

LANGUAGE

Catalan and Spanish (Castilian) are both used in Catalonia, but Catalans will use their own language and will not consider it rude to speak it among themselves when someone who only speaks Castilian is present. It is now taught as the first language in schools. All signs are in Catalan, as are most guidebooks and information notices. The following phrases, first in Catalan, then Spanish, may help:

Good morning	*Bon dia, Buenos días*
Good evening	*Bona tarda, Buenas tardes*
Hello	*Hola, Hola*
Goodbye	*Adéu, Adiós*
Please	*Si us plau, Por favor*
Thank you	*Gracies, Merci gracias*
You're welcome	*De res, De nada*
How much is...?	*¿quant val…? ¿cuanto es…?*
Where is the lavatory?	*¿on és el lavabo? ¿donde esta el lavabo?*
The police station	*la policia, la policia*
The doctor	*el metge, el medéco*
At what time?	*¿quina hora? ¿que hora?*
Open	*Obert, Abierto*
Closed	*Tancat, Cerrado*

Numbers

Catalan:	*un, dos, tres, quatre, cinc, sis, set, vuit, nou, deu.*
Castilian:	*uno, dos, tres, cuatro, cinco, seis, siete, ocho, nueve, diez.*

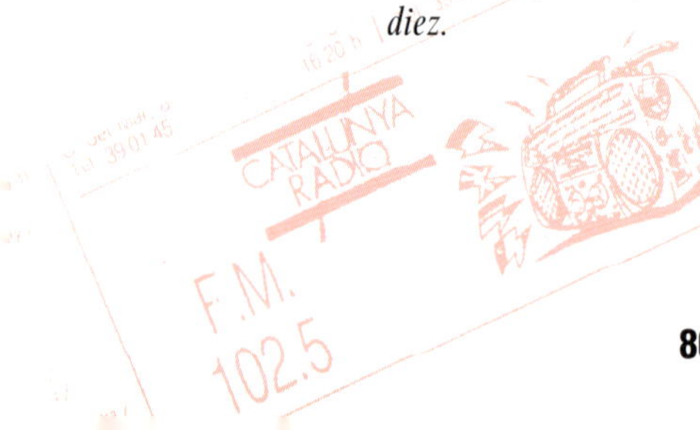

Eating Out

Many restaurants have inexpensive set menus for around 900 pesetas. Expect to pay about 2,000 pesetas for a substantial *à la carte*, including house wine, which is invariably preferable to a gamble on an expensive wine list. The following Catalan words might help when trying to decipher a menu:

Entrats	**First course**
amanida	salad
anxoves	anchovies
bolet	mushroom
cargol	snail
fideus	pasta
truita	omelette
pernil	ham
pastís	terrine
Verdures	**Vegetables**
all	garlic
bledes	chard
nap	turnip
pebrots	sweet peppers
pésols	peas
Peix i Mariscs	**Fish and Shellfish**
bacallà	salt cod
calamars	squid
gambes	prawns
llagosta	lobster
lluç	hake
musclos	mussels
peix espasa	swordfish
pop	octopus
rap	monkfish
tonyina	tuna
truita (de riu)	trout
Carn	**Meat**
ànec	duck
cabrot	goat
botifarra	pork sausage
bou	beef
conill	rabbit
faisà	pheasant
fetge	liver
guatlla	quail
llom	chop
senglar	boar
tripa	tripe
vedella	veal

xai	lamb
Postres	**Pudding**
crema catalana	a local *crème brûlée*
flam crema catalana	out of a small tub
formatge	cheese
fruits secs	nuts and dried fruit
gelat	ice cream
mel i mató	cream cheese and honey
Les Fruites	**Fruit**
ananàs	pineapple
figues	figs
peres	pears
poma	apple
préssec	peach
taronja	orange
raïm	grapes

Train and Bus

Castilian is a better bet, as the ticket vendor may not be from the region:

When is the next train/bus to..? *¿Cuando sale el próximo tren/autobus para...*

How much? *¿Cuanto es?*

Single *Ida*

Return *Ida y vuelta*

COMMUNICATION & MEDIA

Post

Stamps are sold at tobacconists (*tabac*). Post abroad can take from four days to a fortnight. There is a fast delivery service called 'Express'. Mail sent to you for collection at a post office should be marked: *Lista de Correos*.

Telephone

Five and 25 peseta coins can be used for local calls, and a minimum of 15 pesetas is needed. For overseas calls use 100-peseta coins: at least three will be needed just to get through. There are more convenient cabins, some installed temporarily in summer, where you can phone first and pay afterwards. All public phone boxes have

clear instructions in English, French and German about international dialling. First dial 07, followed by the country's code; 44 to the UK, 353 for Eire, 33 for France, 49 for Germany, 61 for Australia, 1 for Canada and the USA.

The code for Girona province is 72. From the UK first dial the code for Spain: 01034. From any other province in Spain, first dial 9. From the Costa Brava call Barcelona numbers by first dialling 93.

Media

There are a seven television channels in the region, both public and private, two in Catalan. Satellite television is gaining ground and many hotels have dishes. A radio service for holidaymakers can be found on 105MHz on the FM band. Each day at 10.30am it broadcasts an hour in English, followed by an hour in German, an hour in Italian and an hour in French.

Girona has two daily papers, *Diari de Girona* and *El Punt*, both in Catalan. In summer they sometimes publish listings of events in several languages. Other multi-lingual publications spring up in the summer months, such as *Publintur*. The local tourist offices also have regular publications detailing events.

GETTING AROUND

Train

Although train journeys are inexpensive, the two lines of the national RENFE network going through the province are not very helpful as they only touch the coast beyond Blanes at Malgrat de Mar in the south, and at Llançà in the north. The line to Ripoll, Puigcerdà and, eventually, Toulouse, the R2, goes from Barcelona.

A Tranvía is a local train, second-class only, which stops at most stations. An Expreso or Rapido stops only at the main stations. The Talgo is a luxury express.

Bus

There are both regular local buses and special summer services connecting the resorts and main towns. Timetables may be posted in the town hall or nearest shop or café window. Day excursions are also organised from the main resorts. Sarfa is the main private operator on the coast. Buses go from Plaça Duc de Medinaceli 4 (near the Drassanes Metro station) in Barcelona. The bus station adjoins the RENFE station in Girona.

Car

The main car hire firms operate in the principal areas, but local firms are often cheaper. There is a high tax on rental, which makes it expensive. Driving licence and passport are required and a deposit may be asked for.

Motorists need a bail bond, which insurance companies often issue without being asked when applying for a green card for travel in Spain. It prevents automatic incarceration in the event of an accident. An international driving licence is not necessary. A warning triangle, nationality sticker, spare set of bulbs and seat belts are obligatory.

Boat Trips

Boats regularly sail in summer from Tamariu to Blanes. These are run by Cruceros Costa Brava, based in Palamós, and the glass-bottomed Panoramic of Lineas Azules SA. Boats also leave regularly from L'Estartit to the Medes Islands (see Tour 5).

ACCOMMODATION

If you plan to stay in a resort in July or August, booking is strongly advised. Many hotels are closed between November and March. Local tourist offices have lists of all accommodation.

Hotels

There are some 1,000 hotels, with around 85,000 beds, in the province, ranging from the luxurious 5-star Gavina in S'Agaro to the humble *fonda*, for centuries the mainstay of travellers in Spain. An *Hostal* displays an H, and is slightly cheaper than a hotel. HR mean Hotel-Residència, an establishment without dining facilities. An evening meal is not obligatory with a hotel room. Prices are posted in the bedrooms. The traditional categories, such as *fonda*, *pensió* and *hostal* are, however, being phased out, and a straight star system, one to five, is being introduced.

Apartments

Flats and villas are frequently advertised in the press, and local tourist offices (see 'Useful Addresses') have lists of agents. Prices are usually inclusive of water and light, but a deposit may be required which should not be more than 25 per cent of the total rent. A key rating exists, rather like the hotel star rating, but even a one-key apartment must have hot water and a shower.

Camp Sites

Every resort on the coast has a camp site – some have several. Beneath umbrella pines and beside sandy beaches, they occupy some prime locations: between Sant Feliu and Tossa some coves are given over entirely to camping. There are three categories of camp site, and though not expensive, their prices can be compared with those of a moderate hotel.

Complaints

If you have trouble sorting out any major problems with the owner or manager of the establishment in which you are staying, ask them for a complaints form (*hoja de reclamaciones*) to fill in. The form is in three parts and once it is completed, you keep a copy, the owner/manager keeps a copy and a third copy goes to the tourist authorities.

SPORT

Beach Activities

Swimming is generally safe everywhere, but the large sweep of beaches at Roses and the Platja de Pals do occasionally experience large freak waves. There are waterskiing schools in the larger resorts. Most beaches have fun boats for hire: canoes, pedaloes and windsurf boards. If you are a novice, don't windsurf if there is a strong off-shore wind. Some beaches are patrolled by life guards and Red Cross boats, but don't count on them.

Diving

The coves offer wonderful opportunities for snorkelling and equipment is cheap and abundant in the shops. Serious diving can be undertaken from clubs at a dozen resorts. The most rewarding is L'Estartit, where boats go out to the marine reserve around the Medes Islands all year round. Contact Unisub, Bar Tortuga, Carretera de Torroella, or Medes-Sub, Passeig Marítim. The new reserve around the Ullastres can be dived from the Triton Diving Centre in Plaça dels Pins, Llafranc, or Poseidon-Nemrod, Platja Port Pelegri, Calella de Palafrugell.

Fishing

Sea fishing is popular, and rods and lines are easily bought. River fishing is also possible, but for the best fish, such as trout, you need to go to the clear, fast-running waters near the sources: to the Ter at Camprodón, for example. Licences are inexpensive and issued by the local tourist office.

Golf
To date there are five clubs in the province, with good reputations. Ask for any special weekly or monthly rates. Club de Golf Costa Brava, Santa Cristina d'Aro (Tel: 972-83 71 50/ Fax: 972-83 72 72); Club de Golf Pals (Tel: 972-66 77 40/Fax: 972-66 77 36); Club de Golf Mas Nou, Platja d'Aro (Tel: 972-82 80 84/Fax: 972-82 81 17); Club de Golf Girona, Girona (Tel: 972-22 22 62/Fax: 972-22 12 38); Club de Golf Empordà, Gualta (Tel: 972-76 04 50/76 00 33).

Horse Riding
There is a stable (*club hipic*) at most of the large resorts. Riders tend not to wear hats.

Sailing
Although temporary berths are inexpensive, jetties and harbours become very full in summer. Empúria-brava, Palamós, La Platja d'Aro and Sant Feliu de Guíxols all have safe marinas with full facilities.

Skiing
The skiing season in the Pyrenees can last from January to the beginning of April. There are resorts at Vallter 2000, above Camprodon, and at Vall de Núria above Ripoll. But the best places are the popular La Molina and Masella resorts on the edge of the Cerdanya valley. Further information: Estació d'Esquí La Molina, Avinguda Supermolina s/n, 17573 La Molina-Alp, Girona (Tel: 972-89 20 31).

Walking
Walking is a popular weekend pastime in Catalonia, and there are a number of special routes marked including long-distance GR routes. Shorter walks are marked with red-and-white parallel stripes painted on stones and trees. Tourist offices often have local hand-drawn maps.

WILDLIFE

Conservation is gaining ground in the region, particularly with the establishment of Aiguamolls (see Tour 3: *The Bay of Roses*). Keep a watch out for birds: some beautiful ones are frequently seen including the princely, crested hoopoe, the bright blue bee-eater, which is a large relation of the kingfisher, the sunshine-yellow golden oriole and the cool blue rock thrush. Among the waders the noisy black-winged stilt is easily identified, and in the mountains buzzards fly in flocks while eagles hunt alone.

Red squirrels live in the woods, foot-long, blue-and-green lizards haunt the roadsides and a variety of swallowtail butterflies flit everywhere. In the mountains there are lady orchids, gentian, pasqueflowers. Take photographs, but don't pick them.

There is no danger from creepy crawlies, but there can be irritations. An anti-wasp spray or cream can come in handy, as can mosquito ointment or coils. 'Jellies', plastic sandles, are handy for swimming among rocks where there are sea urchins. Their prickles are a devil to get out.

MUSEUMS

There are a good variety of museums in the region, generally open 9am–1pm and 4–7pm and closed all day Monday and on Sunday afternoon. Entrance fees are modest, usually 100–200 pesetas.

Arbúcies:

MUSEU ETNOLOGIC DEL MONTSENY

A well laid-out exhibition of local crafts and industries, including coach-building.

Banyoles

MUSEU ARQUEOLOGIC COMARCAL

Prehistoric finds including a famous Neanderthal jawbone.

MUSEU DARDER

Anthropology and ethnology, including some grotesque mummies. One ticket buys entry to both.

Figueres

TEATRO-MUSEU DALI

Works and jokes by the artist and some by others. Open all day. Highly popular.

MUSEU DE JOQUETS

In the Rambla; has Spain's largest toy collection.

MUSEU DE L'EMPORDÀ

An oddball, once private collection.

Llagostera

FUNDACIO EMILI VILA

The former family home of a local painter whose *belle époque* work flourished in Paris. Some of his works are for sale. Plus works by Modigliani and a Lautrec self-portrait.

Olot

MUSEU COMARCAL

An impressive museum in the old hospice, with the Olot School well represented. Closed Tuesday.

Peralada

MUSEU-BIBLIOTECA DEL CONVENT DEL CARME

Large collections in its library, wine museum and ceramic room. Regular guided tours.

Ripoll

ARXIU-MUSEU FOLKLORIC

A delightful collection of industrial and rural history.

Sant Hilari Sacalm

MUSEU MUNICIPAL DE LES GUILLERIES

A couple of rooms in the town hall, with stuffed animals and flora from the surrounding hills.

Sils

COL.LECIO D'AUTOMOBILS DE SALVADOR CLARET

Antique car collection.

Torroella de Montgrí

MUSEU DEL MONTGRI I DEL BAIX TER

An exhibition of flora and fauna of the region.

Tossa

MUSEU DE LA VILA VELLA

Paintings by local and European artists, including Chagall.

Ullastret

MUSEU MONOGRÀFIC DEL POBLAT IBERIC

In the grounds of the large Iberian settlement.

Vic

MUSEU EPISCOPAL
Beside the cathedral, it has some magnificent Romanesque paintings and statuary.

Girona City

MUSEU ARQUAEOLOGIC DE SANT PERE DE GALLIGANS
Plaça de Santa Llúcia.
Archaeology from the whole region in fine Romanesque church.

MUSEU CAPITULAR I CLAUSTRES DE LA CATEDRAL
In the cathedral; contains the wonderful 12th-century *Tapestry of the Creation.*

MUSEU D'ART
Palau Epicopal Pujada de la Catedral.
Many church treasures, from early Romanesque to Gothic, plus 20th-century art.

MUSEU DE LA CIUTAT
Carrer de la Força.
A small museum of the city's past, plus a *sardana* collection, in an old Cappuchin convent.

USEFUL ADDRESSES

Tourist Offices

Tourist offices in the main resorts are all well signposted. Letters should be sent to the Oficines de Turisme at the addresses listed (north to south) below. The telephone area code is 72.

Portbou: *Pg de la Sardana, 12.*
Tel: 39 02 84. Fax: 12 51 23.
Llançà: *Av Europa, 37.*
Tel: 38 08 55. Fax: 38 12 58.
Roses: *Av de Rhode, s/n.*
Tel: 25 73 31. Fax: 15 09 96.
L'Escala: *Pl de les Escoles, 1.*
Tel: 77 06 03. Fax: 10 33 85.
L'Estartit: *Pg Marítim, 57.*
Tel: 75 89 10. Fax: 75 76 19.
Begur: *Av Onze de Sepembre s/n.*
Tel: 62 34 69. Fax: 62 35 88.
Palafrugell: *Carrilet, 2.*
Tel: 30 02 28. Fax: 61 12 61.
Palamós: *Pg del Mar s/n.*
Tel: 31 43 90. Fax: 31 61 10.
Platja d'Aro: *Mn J. Verdaguer, 11.*
Tel: 81 71 79. Fax: 82 56 57.
Sant Feliu de Guíxols: *Pl Monastir, 54. Tel: 82 00 51. Fax: 82 01 19.*
Tossa de Mar: *Cra Lloret de Mar.*
Tel: 34 01 08. Fax: 34 07 12.
Lloret de Mar: *Pl de la Vila, 1.*
Tel: 36 47 35. Fax: 36 77 50.
Blanes: *Pl Catalunya s/n.*
Tel: 33 03 48. Fax: 33 46 86.
Girona: *Rambla de la Libertat, 1.*
Tel: 41 94 19. Fax: 41 94 18.
Banyoles: *Pg Indústria, 25.*
Tel: 57 55 73. Fax: 57 49 17.
Olot: *Lorenzana, 15.*
Tel: 26 01 41. Fax: 27 00 56.

Consulates

The nearest are in Barcelona:
UK: *Av Diagonal 447.*
Tel: (93) 419 90 44.
Ireland: *Gran Via Carles III, 94.*
Tel: (93) 330 98 52.
USA: *Gran Via Carles III, 33.*
Tel: (93) 280 22 27.

Spanish Tourist Offices Abroad

In the UK the Spanish National Tourist Office is at 27–58 St James's Street, London SW1 1LD, Tel: 071-499 1901. In North America there are offices in Chicago (312) 944 0215; Los Angeles (213) 658 7188; Miami (305) 536 1222; New York (212) 759 8822 and Toronto (416) 961 3131.

A typical Costa Brava coastline

Index

A

B

C

D, E

F

G

H, I, J

L

S

T, U

V, Z

Art & Photo Credits

Photography	**Roger Williams** *and*
17B, 20, 21, 22, 38, 68, 71	**AGE Fotostock**
67	**Tor Eigeland**
Cover, 10/11, 13, 18, 37, 41, 61	**Bill Wassman**
Cover Design	**Klaus Geisler**
Cartography	**Berndtson & Berndtson**

INSIGHT GUIDES

COLORSET NUMBERS

160 Alaska
155 Alsace
150 Amazon Wildlife
116 America, South
173 American Southwest
158A Amsterdam
260 Argentina
287 Asia, East
207 Asia, South
262 Asia, South East
194 Asian Wildlife, Southeast
167A Athens
272 Australia
263 Austria
188 Bahamas
206 Bali Baru
107 Baltic States
246A Bangkok
292 Barbados
219B Barcelona
187 Bay of Naples
234A Beijing
109 Belgium
135A Berlin
217 Bermuda
100A Boston
127 Brazil
178 Brittany
109A Brussels
144A Budapest
260A Buenos Aires
213 Burgundy
268A Cairo
247B Calcutta
275 California
180 California, Northern
161 California, Southern
237 Canada
162 Caribbean The Lesser Antilles
122 Catalonia (Costa Brava)
141 Channel Islands
184C Chicago
151 Chile
234 China
135E Cologne
119 Continental Europe
189 Corsica
281 Costa Rica
291 Cote d'Azur
165 Crete
184 Crossing America
226 Cyprus
114 Czechoslovakia
247A Delhi, Jaipur, Agra
238 Denmark
135B Dresden
142B Dublin
135F Düsseldorf
204 East African Wildlife
149 Eastern Europe,
118 Ecuador
148A Edinburgh
268 Egypt
123 Finland
209B Florence
243 Florida
154 France
135C Frankfurt
208 Gambia & Senegal
135 Germany
148B Glasgow
279 Gran Canaria
169 Great Barrier Reef
124 Great Britain
167 Greece
166 Greek Islands
135G Hamburg
240 Hawaii
193 Himalaya, Western
196 Hong Kong
144 Hungary
256 Iceland
247 India
212 India, South
128 Indian Wildlife
143 Indonesia
142 Ireland
252 Israel
236A Istanbul
209 Italy
213 Jamaica
278 Japan
266 Java
252A Jerusalem-Tel Aviv
203A Kathmandu
270 Kenya
300 Korea
202A Lisbon
258 Loire Valley
124A London
275A Los Angeles
201 Madeira
219A Madrid
145 Malaysia
157 Mallorca & Ibiza
117 Malta
272B Melbourne
285 Mexico
285A Mexico City
243A Miami
237B Montreal
235 Morocco
101A Moscow
135D Munich
211 Myanmar (Burma)
259 Namibia
269 Native America
203 Nepal
158 Netherlands
100 New England
184E New Orleans
184F New York City
133 New York State
293 New Zealand
265 Nile, The
120 Norway
124B Oxford
147 Pacific Northwest
205 Pakistan
154A Paris
249 Peru
184B Philadelphia
222 Philippines
115 Poland
202 Portugal
114A Prague
153 Provence
156 Puerto Rico
250 Rajasthan
177 Rhine
127A Rio de Janeiro
172 Rockies
209A Rome
101 Russia
275B San Francisco
130 Sardinia
148 Scotland
184D Seattle
261 Sicily
159 Singapore
257 South Africa
264 South Tyrol
219 Spain
220 Spain, Southern
105 Sri Lanka
101B St Petersburg
170 Sweden
232 Switzerland
272 Sydney
175 Taiwan
112 Tenerife
186 Texas
246 Thailand
278A Tokyo
139 Trinidad & Tobago
113 Tunisia
236 Turkey
171 Turkish Coast
210 Tuscany
174 Umbria
237A Vancouver
198 Venezuela
209C Venice
263A Vienna
255 Vietnam
267 Wales
184C Washington DC
183 Waterways of Europe
215 Yemen

You'll find the colorset number on the spine of each Insight Guide.